STENCILLING

A Design and Source Book

STENCILLING
A Design and Source Book

Edited by
BRIDGET FRASER
Introduction by ADELE BISHOP

PHOTOGRAPHY BY DAVID ARKY AND OTHERS

HENRY HOLT AND COMPANY, NEW YORK

ACKNOWLEDGMENTS

The Miller Press and Jane Ross Associates would like to express their immense gratitude to the following people for their help in bringing this book into being:

To Adele Bishop and Cile Lord who shared their discoveries of using fast-drying japan paints and transparent stencil material in their book, *The Art of Decorative Stenciling,* and who have consulted with us at every step. To Cile Lord for taking the trouble to read and check the entire text.

To Lynn Goodpasture and Kate Williams who, having learned from Adele and Cile's authority, have become professional stencillers and have devised more ideas and shortcuts of their own, which they have generously shared with us throughout the progress of the book. To Kate we would like to express our appreciation for her help with the material on color and design; her expertise has added substantially to our text, and her studio has been a constant source of ideas. To Lynn again, for sharing her expertise and ideas, for opening up her home for many of our shoots, and for her great patience while we took over. We'd also like to thank Lynn and Kate for making available photographs from their portfolios.

To Virginia Teichner for introducing us to her clients and arranging for us to invade their homes and take pictures of unique work which they commissioned. We are indebted to Vera Goldman, Linda Donn, and Trish Mendenhall for allowing us to photograph Virginia's stencilling. Thanks also to Virginia for letting us photograph the samples of her portfolio.

To Kari McCabe of McBride & Associates (New York) and Vincent P. De Luca for allowing us to stencil and photograph the floor in Mr. De Luca's apartment, which forms part of Kari's design for the whole apartment.

To Tom Burgio for sharing with us tricks of the trade that he developed over the years. To Kathie Marron-Wall for producing beautiful work from a distance. To Mary MacCarthy over in England who worked at an even greater distance and who shared her home and work with us. To Carolyn Warrender, also in England, who shared so many decorating ideas with us.

To Margaret Lucas at the Cooper-Hewitt Museum Library for help in researching the foundations of the project.

To Min Hogg and Nicolette le Pelley at *The World of Interiors* for leading us to British artists and lending us their pictures.

To Ellen Garbarino at the Society for the Preservation of New England Antiquities for showing us Moses Eaton's work and equipment and for lending us transparencies.

To Pat Thayer at Stencil-Ease and Bob Paul at Adele Bishop Inc.; to Arthur Brown & Brothers artists' materials stores and Laura Ashley Inc., who all supplied us with props for the photographs.

To Virginia Croft for her painstaking work on our manuscript.

To Sallie Baldwin and her team at Antler & Baldwin Design Group, especially Lisa Greenfield and Hugo Sarago, for their design and wonderful "touches."

To Meryl Henderson who expertly drew the instructional diagrams for the projects.

To David Arky and John Vere Brown for their wonderful photography.

And to those too numerous to mention who helped.

First published in February 1987 by
Henry Holt and Company, Inc., 521 Fifth Avenue,
New York, New York 10175.
Produced by The Miller Press, Inc. and
Jane Ross Associates, Inc.

Distributed in Canada by Fitzhenry & Whiteside,
195 Allstate Parkway, Markham, Ontario L3R 4T8.

Library of Congress Cataloging-in-Publication Data
Stencilling: a design and source book.
    Bibliography: p.
    Includes index.
    1. Stencil work—Technique. I. Fraser, Bridget.
NK8654.S74 1987   745.7′3   86-9959
            ISBN 0-8050-0108-5

First Edition
DESIGNED BY THE ANTLER & BALDWIN DESIGN GROUP
Printed in the United States of America

10 9 8 7 6 5 4 3 2 1

ISBN 0-8050-0108-5

Contents

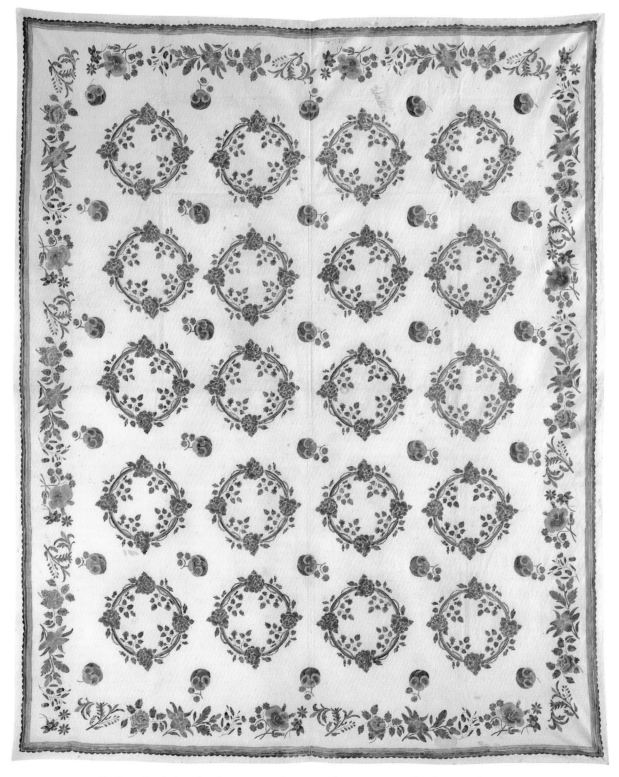

An antique stencilled quilt dating back to 1867. Strong colors were applied to a white cotton background to produce an extraordinarily sophisticated effect. *Courtesy America Hurrah, New York.*

Introduction

If you have glanced through the pages of this book and it has captured your imagination, you are probably eager to undertake one of its projects. Unlike many artistic mediums, stencilling does not require countless hours of training before you will be able to create lovely things. This, in part, accounts for its enormous popularity today, for both the hobbyist and the professional decorator. By mastering a few basic techniques, you will find that triumphs in stencilling are possible and you may discover creative abilities you did not realize you possessed.

There are many historical examples of stencilling used for a variety of purposes by civilizations having little in common other than a need to create pattern. In ancient China, for instance, a system of stencilling was used for the purpose of printing countless images of the Buddha. The more replicas of this holy being a Buddhist monk could produce in a lifetime, the holier he believed himself to be. In Peru, exotic designs on ritualistic robes found buried in the Nazca Desert were actually stencilled on the fabric. Ancient Japanese artisans elevated stencilling to an art form. Their sensitivity to beauty and exquisite detail is unparalleled in history. In Europe, before the advent of the printing press, the illustrations for books and playing cards were reproduced by stencilling, with fine detail added by hand afterward.

Today we are experiencing what some people like to call "the great stencilling revival." I believe that stencilling emerges in response to changes in fashions and lifestyles. The voluptuous clutter of Victorian stencilling gave way to the more graceful, flowing style of Art Nouveau and Art Deco. Today stencilling is re-emerging as we pursue yet another very different style known as the "country look." Could its guileless, down-to-earth, often whimsical qualities be an antidote to the awesome complexity of today's lifestyles?

More than fifty years ago a remarkable woman named Janet Waring stumbled on an art form that lay virtually buried and ignored. Her years of diligent research into stencilling resulted in a book published in the 1930s on early American wall stencils. It was appreciated by a handful of scholars, at best. Many years later, long after the book was out of print, a well-known photographer, Ernst Beadle, loaned me his precious copy of Janet Waring's book. From the moment I opened the pages, I knew the direction my life would take. Convinced these designs were what the world needed, I set out to "spread the word," but the timing was not right. The decorating world was not ready. Unfazed, I looked for another way to promote interest in stencilled decorative patterns. After experimenting with new materials and methods for creating intricate, non-stencil-like designs, I invited Cile Lord to join forces with me.

We formed a partnership in 1963 in what was to become the most imaginative, marvelously creative adventure anyone could hope to have. We began a custom stencilling business known as Bishop & Lord. It was exhilarating to have the field all to ourselves! The more intricate and lavish our designs, the greater was the challenge. To the media, we were irresistible, and they launched our new creative venture with headlines such as "Bishop & Lord . . . are a team of stencilers whose devotion to decorated surface is only slightly less than was Michelangelo's" (*Newsday*).

Suddenly something happened we were not prepared for. In 1966 *House and Garden* magazine invited us to execute a project with "how-to" instructions for their readers. Until this time we had kept the materials and techniques we used a closely guarded secret. (Cile and I didn't want anyone to know how we performed our magic!) Because the publicity would be sensational, however, we went ahead with the project and, soon after, began to receive inquiries about where these wonderful materials might be located. In the early 1970s the allure of stencilling prompted Cile and me to write a book on our stencilling methods. It took us two years to prepare and was held by the publisher two more years to await the Bicentennial of 1976. Our book, *The Art of Decorative Stenciling* (New York, Viking Press, 1976), for the first time disclosed the methods and materials we had so closely guarded during the wonderful years that we had worked together.

Meanwhile, I had moved to Vermont to live, while Cile continued with the custom stencilling business in New York. During the years in Vermont, my involvement with stencilling took another direction. My husband and I wanted to make stencilling accessible to everyone who wanted to learn. We started a small mail-order business to make the proper materials available. I created a teaching program to train serious students who wanted to stencil beautifully and who

would, in turn, go out and teach others. My husband and I consolidated the mail-order business with the training program to reinforce our original goals. Many students graduated to begin stencilling careers for themselves.

Popular interest in stencilling was mushrooming, and other companies began to offer stencil materials. Cile and I saw many of our standards modified in order to reach a wider audience. Precut stencils were promoted. Less emphasis was placed on the quality of brushes and paints, and more "gimmicky" materials were introduced. The accessibility of stencilling had grown by leaps and bounds and reached thousands who enjoyed it as a hobby.

Fortunately, there continued to be a few stencil artists who contributed in a beautiful and creative way to the world of stencilling. Because of their generous talents and persevering efforts, stencilling has continued to flower in the home-decorating field as well as the craft and hobby field, not only in America but also in Europe. It is becoming one of the most fashionable ways of introducing pattern to our homes. This new breadth of application allows stencilling to encompass much more as an artistic expression.

I am greatly pleased the publisher and editors have made this book a reality. Each of the eight stencil artists herein has made a special contribution to his or her field of stencilling. The reader is sure to be inspired by the selection of stencil projects, which serve as excellent examples of good design. This book deserves recognition for presenting stencilling at its best.

ADELE BISHOP 1986

About the Artists

Tom Burgio, who earned a bachelors degree in art education at Monmouth College, New Jersey, began stencilling professionally in 1976 when he joined Stencil Magic, originators of the first precut plastic stencils. There he was part of a three-man design team whose work appeared frequently in home and crafts magazines. Tom traveled widely on behalf of Stencil Magic, giving workshops to various groups such as craft retailers and cable TV viewers. Because many new manufacturers began to offer stencilling supplies, in 1984 Tom developed Stencil World, a unique mail-order catalog expressly devoted to the craft. He also designs in other crafts, notably lace panels, for which he created the mail-order company Chelsea Lace Place.

Lynn Goodpasture, whose early training was in pastel portraiture, sculpture, and drawing, has been stencilling professionally for ten years, designing and executing projects for designers, architects, and home owners. She works in all period styles of decor, as well as contemporary design. In addition to stencilling, Lynn executes marbleized, gold leaf, and other painted finishes and handpaints on walls, floors, ceilings, furniture, fabric, and floorcloths. Her work appears in homes, office buildings, hotels, stores, and restaurants. On occasion Lynn teaches the craft of stencilling privately and at museums, most notably the Cooper Hewitt in New York. Her studio is located in New York City.

Cile Lord began her professional stencilling career in 1963, when she and Adele Bishop formed the partnership of Bishop & Lord in New York. She earned a masters degree in painting at the University of Iowa, after studying at Baylor University, the Hoffman School, and Prang Textile Studios. Co-author, with Adele Bishop, of *The Art of Decorative Stenciling,* today she continues to create and execute stencilled designs on commission in her studio in New York. A successful painter as well, she has been awarded a MacDowell Fellowship and exhibits in New York City and East Hampton, Long Island, where she makes her home.

Mary MacCarthy, after training in textile design at London's Camberwell School of Art, visited the United States for six months in 1972. Her encounter with American folk art, including stencilling, impressed her greatly, and on returning to England she set up her own stencilling business. Her many varied commissions have taken her to New York and Spain as well as throughout England, working both independently and in collaboration with some of Europe's top decorators. Her work has been featured in *House and Garden* in the United States and *The World of Interiors* in England. Her home is in Stiffkey, on the north Norfolk coast.

Kathie Marron-Wall comes from an extensive art background in New York. She studied at Marymount College and the Institute of Fine Arts, New York University, before working in the art departments of several publishing houses and advertising firms. Sixteen years ago she moved to Dorset, Vermont, where she became Adele Bishop's assistant and her first master teacher. She has taught more than 1500 students throughout the United States, Canada, and England. Kathie has stencilled rooms throughout New England and has restored antique stencilled rooms, many of which have appeared in magazines. She also continues to teach in her studio in Dorset.

Virginia Teichner trained at the Art Students League in New York and shortly thereafter opened her own stencilling design firm, which is based in Connecticut. For the past twelve years she has worked extensively throughout New York and Connecticut. Although most of her work has been done in private homes, she also has carried out stencilling projects for Bloomingdale's, W&J Sloane's, and various other decorator showcases. Recently she was involved in the restoration of the stencilling in Battell Chapel at Yale University. Traditional custom designs are her hallmark.

Carolyn Warrender started her career as an interior designer with the distinguished British interior design company, Colefax and Fowler. Her formal education in art, coupled with the influence of John Fowler's predilection for painted surfaces, led her to the idea of starting her own business specializing in decorating with stencils. Following an extensive study of American folk art in New England, Carolyn founded her now thriving Chelsea-based interior design company and shop, Stencil Designs Ltd., the first of its kind in England. Her clients can either create their own stencilled decorative schemes or have a professional do it for them, and in the shop they can purchase American stencilling materials.

Kate Williams is a prominent New York stencil artist, as well as a designer of wallpaper and textiles for several well-known manufacturers. After formal training at the Pennsylvania Academy of Fine Arts and the University of Pennsylvania, she came to New York to pursue a career as a painter. Her enthusiasm for stencilling led to her accepting design commissions a few years ago, and today she does a considerable amount of interior decoration involving original stencil designs for private clients. Her studio and home are located in Manhattan.

A stencilling kit that belonged to Moses Eaton, Jr. (1796–1886) of Hancock, New Hampshire, and an example of a wall stencil executed by him. *Courtesy Society for the Preservation of New England Antiquities. Photo by J. David Bohl.*

Opposite page: The magical effect of this modern screen was created by stencilling over a sponged background. *Courtesy Pavilion, Edinburgh, Scotland.*

10

CHAPTER ONE
Materials & Techniques

Stencilling is a wonderfully versatile and accessible craft. Whether you are artistic or simply appreciate attractive and interesting decorative effects, you can easily learn this rewarding hobby. Once you are familiar with the materials and have practiced the techniques, you will be able to stencil almost anything you choose and achieve beautiful, long-lasting results.

In stencilling, as in any new craft or skill, you should begin by familiarizing yourself with the basic equipment required and learn how to use it. Take the time to acquaint yourself with all the materials and techniques of stencilling before undertaking any of the projects in this book. Even though stencilling is an almost foolproof art, your results will always be much better if you thoroughly understand what you are doing and why.

When you look at the picture at left of Moses Eaton's stencilling equipment, which dates back to the early eighteenth century, and compare it to the basic equipment used today, you might be surprised to see how little has changed. The brushes, the stencils, the cutting knife—all are virtually the same now as they were then.

In the past twenty years, however, with the resurgence of interest in stencilling, several developments have contributed to a complete transformation of the craft, broadening its appeal and permitting an infinite number of design possibilities. The most important of these was Adele Bishop's development of the use of Mylar®, a transparent acetate film, for making stencils. Acetate allows the stenciller to see not only the surface beneath the stencil but also previously stencilled forms. It also eliminates the need for painstaking registration marking, which used to be a major obstacle for the unskilled stenciller.

There have also been important developments in the manufacture of paint. Fast-drying japan and acrylic paints make the stenciller's job much easier, eliminating the danger of smudging and speeding up the process. Paints have also been devised for a wider variety of surfaces. Fabric and ceramic stencilling are now simple tasks with long-lasting results.

Another modern miracle, the photocopier, has simplified the drawing of designs and stencil outlines and has eased the not-so-skilled draftsman's task dramatically. Now almost any outline or design is accessible to anyone. Photocopiers or photostat machines can enlarge or floors to textiles. Stencil outlines are drawn on the acetate with permanent or india ink and will not wash off once they have dried. Errors must be removed immediately with a damp tissue. Acetate stencils can be cleaned easily with turpentine if japan color is used. Although water will remove wet acrylic paint, it is hard to dissolve when dry.

Sheets of acetate are available at art-supply stores and usually measure approximately 24 inches by 36 inches. Buy acetate by the sheet rather than by the roll and transport it home flat if possible. If you buy it by the roll, you may have difficulty making it lie flat. Always draw, cut, and stencil on the side of the acetate that bends away from you when it hangs free.

MYLAR® Mylar is the trade name for a brand of plastic film similar to acetate and is the material Adele Bishop used in her line of stencil kits. It has a slightly frosted appearance but is sufficiently transparent to see through and to trace through. Its advantage over regular acetate is that the frosted surface can be drawn on with pencil. You can draw your stencil outlines on the dull side and stencil from the shiny side. Mylar is available at art-supply stores and comes in a range of grades: .004 or .005 is best for making stencils. Both japan color and acrylic paint can be used with Mylar.

WAXED STENCIL PAPER Light and intricate stencilling is often done with waxed stencil paper, which is a strong paper coated with a heavy layer of wax on each side. (Do not confuse it with culinary waxed paper.) It is not sufficiently durable for wall and floor stencilling, but is suitable for small projects because it is easier to manipulate than acetate. Neither pencil nor ink will take on the waxed surface, and so it is necessary to cut the stencils directly from an outline placed underneath the paper, which is semi-transparent. Waxed stencil paper is sold by the sheet or roll at art-supply stores.

OAKTAG Oaktag is a heavy grade of paper stock, widely available in both art-supply stores and stationery stores. It resembles the stencil materials of the past and is relatively durable, is easy to cut, and can be drawn on with pencil and ink. Its main drawback is that it is opaque, making registration more difficult. You can use oaktag successfully for stencilling greeting cards or wrapping paper when only one stencil is involved and no complicated registration is required. To make it more durable you can coat it on both sides with polyurethane varnish.

TECHNICAL DRAWING PEN OR FELT-TIP MARKER PEN A Rapidograph or permanent felt-tip marker pen is best for drawing on acetate. Make sure you use permanent ink that does not dissolve in either water or turpentine when dry, and a fine nib.

UTILITY KNIFE A Stanley® knife or similar utility or mat knife is best for cutting acetate stencils. It should not be too cumbersome, but strong enough to cut the acetate. For cutting waxed paper or Mylar® stencils, an X-acto® knife or similar paper scalpel will suffice. You may find the blade of an X-acto® useful for cutting fine points in acetate too. Always have plenty of spare blades and replace them frequently. Cutting blades should be fine, not heavy-duty.

GLASS CUTTING MAT A sheet of plain glass approximately 12 inches by 12 inches and ¼ inch thick is the best surface on which to cut acetate or Mylar® stencils. Have the edges of the glass filed or tape them so that you will not cut yourself. For larger stencils, such as for a floor, you may need a larger piece of glass. Paint the underside of the glass white so that the stencil outlines on the acetate show up. This glass plate may also come in handy as a palette on which to mix your paints. If you prefer, you can use a "self-healing" cutting mat, which has a surface that closes up immediately after cutting. The only drawback is that the knife tends to drag more than on a glass cutting mat.

ILLUSTRATION BOARD Artists' illustration board is used in making waxed paper stencils. The standard size is 30 by 40 inches.

MASKING TAPE Masking tape, either 1 inch or ¾ inch wide, is used whenever you wish to anchor your stencil. Buy good-quality tape that retains its stickiness. When tracing a design from paper onto acetate, use masking tape to hold the paper and the acetate together.

CLEAR TAPE You can use clear tape to repair a stencil when you have overcut or accidentally slipped with the blade or when it has broken with use. Slightly frosted tape (Scotch® brand) is more suitable than completely transparent tape.

FOR MEASURING THE AREA TO BE STENCILLED

MEASURING TOOLS Both a 5-foot metal measuring tape and a dressmaker's cloth tape are useful for measuring and marking the surface to be stencilled, or you may prefer a wooden or metal yardstick. You will also need rulers, a T-square, and a right angle.

PLUMB LINE AND CHALK BOX This comprises a long, extendable string with a loop on one end and a weighted chalk box at the other. The string winds into the box, collecting nonpermanent blue or white chalk dust as it goes. (Do not use permanent chalk.) The string is used to mark straight lines on walls and floors. When it is pulled out tight and snapped, it leaves a clearly defined straight line on the wall or floor surface. Plumb lines are available at hardware stores.

SPIRIT LEVEL This straightedge has a glass-enclosed liquid containing a bubble, which, when centered, indicates the true level on a surface.

PENCILS Both chalk and lead pencils are used for marking points on surfaces to be stencilled. Conté pencils are useful for marking canvas.

KNEADED ERASER Have a kneaded eraser handy for removing incorrect pencil or chalk lines and paint smudges on the surface. It can also be used to lift paint from a newly applied print to create highlights. This is also known sometimes as a putty eraser.

FOR PREPARING BACKGROUNDS

PRODUCTION PAPER OR SANDPAPER A variety of medium to fine grades of sandpaper is necessary for smoothing wooden and other rough surfaces.

Clockwise from top left: **Foam rubber paintbrushes, paint thinner (mineral spirits), shellac primer, spray varnish, tack cloth, flat paintbrushes, small paintbrushes, different grades of sandpaper, polyurethane varnish.** *Photo by David Arky.*

PRIMER All untreated wooden surfaces should be sealed with one or two coats of oil-based primer, which is available at paint and hardware stores.

WALL AND FLOOR PAINTS Apply paints in your chosen colors as backgrounds to your stencilling. Whether you are using an oil-based or water-based paint, choose a flat (matte) or semi-gloss finish. Stencilling will not take successfully on a glossy surface.

STAINS On floors or other wooden surfaces,

you may choose to use a stain rather than an opaque paint. Stains come in a wide range of shades and are applied before stencilling.

PAINTBRUSHES Use flat bristle or nylon paintbrushes for applying background colors. A 2-inch brush is a good all-purpose brush, but you may find you need a selection of sizes. Inexpensive brushes made of foam rubber are also useful for applying paint, stain, or varnish. It is best to use a fresh sponge brush for each medium or color.

SOLVENTS Depending on whether you are using oil- or water-based paint, you will need a good supply of either turpentine, mineral spirits, or water to thin the paint and clean brushes.

TACK CLOTH This is a special cloth designed to pick up dust. Newly sanded wood floors and furniture should be wiped with a tack cloth before painting and varnishing.

MASK When you are working with strong paints and solvents or with quantities of dust, it is a good idea to wear a disposable mask over your nose and mouth. These are available at hardware stores.

FOR APPLYING THE STENCILS

STENCIL BRUSHES Stencil brushes come in a wide range of sizes and grades. The best brushes are made of natural hog bristles. Although expensive, these brushes will last for years and will permit the greatest variety of painting techniques. Black or gray hog bristles are soft and durable. White bristles are firmer and hence less versatile, but they are effective for floor stencilling where a brush gets a lot of heavy-duty use. There are also synthetic bristle brushes on the market that are considerably cheaper, but you will have difficulty achieving the masterful painting that a pure bristle brush permits. Stencil brushes come with either long or short handles. For most of your work, short handles are probably best, but this is a matter of preference.

Brushes will be your major expense in stencilling, and it pays to have a good selection from the start. It is best to work with one brush for each color, in sizes corresponding to the type of

Clockwise from bottom center: **Japan paint, turpentine, paper stencil proof, tubes of artists' oil paint, palette knife and saucer of paint, japan paint, open pots of mixed japan paints, acrylic paints, textile paints, japan paint.** *Center:* **kneaded eraser and long- and short-handled stencil brushes in five sizes.** *Photo by David Arky.*

stencilling. Use large sizes (up to 2 inches) if you have large areas to cover and smaller sizes (½ to ¾ inch) for smaller areas. Always clean and care for your brushes; they are a lifetime investment. Many stencillers recommend the stencil brushes that are made in Germany.

JAPAN COLORS OR PAINTS We recommend you use this paint for stencilling on floors, walls, furniture, and other hard surfaces. Japan color is particularly fast-drying, making it possible to stencil progressively over a surface without any serious danger of the paint smudging. Using japan colors was integral to Adele Bishop's and Cile Lord's successful revival of the art of stencilling. The combination of acetate stencils and japan colors has made mastery of the craft possible for virtually anyone.

Japan paints come in a wide range of colors and are available at art-supply stores or by mail. Mail-order japan colors, which are produced specifically for stencilling, are available in more ready-mixed colors than the basic paints sold at art-supply stores, whose color range is closer to standard artists' colors. The colors listed for the projects in this book refer to the basic japan colors and not the ready-mixed shades. Color names may vary from one brand to another. Japan colors can be mixed with small quantities of artists' oil paint to achieve subtle hues, or they can be mixed freely together to achieve a desired color.

Japan colors are usually sold in cans, starting with ½-pint quantities. You may not use an entire can of the paint in a stencilling project, but you can seal it securely and save the paint for a later project. For this reason, only the color of paint and not the exact quantity is listed in the materials for each project. You will very rarely need more than half a pint of one particular color in a project.

ARTISTS' OILS Small quantities of artists' oil paints are useful for tinting japan colors to subtle hues that may not be available ready mixed. One tube of paint will last a long time, since only a dab is needed for tinting, and therefore only color names, not quantities, are quoted in the materials for a project.

ACRYLIC PAINTS Made from a water base, acrylic paints are as fast-drying as japan colors. They come in a wide range of colors and can be mixed with one another to achieve an even greater range. However, they are not as durable as japan colors and therefore are not so suitable for floors and walls. Also, you cannot achieve the subtle shading effects that are possible with japan colors. As acrylic paint dries, it forms a tough skin, which is desirable on surfaces where an extra-smooth finish is required, such as the small wooden boxes in Chapter 4. However, the skin also forms on brushes and stencils and is hard to remove, so care must be taken to clean them frequently. Acrylics may distort acetate stencils and untreated paper stencils because of the water content of the paint. They are best used with waxed paper stencils and inexpensive brushes and are ideal for stencilling on stationery. Acrylic paints are available at art-supply stores or through mail order.

TEXTILE PAINTS There are various paints on the market today designed specifically for painting on fabric. These paints are fast-drying and will not wash off or disintegrate with careful dry cleaning. Textile paints can be either water- or turpentine-soluble. The water-soluble pigments lose their solubility when treated with a hot iron. The heat of the iron bonds them into the fabric fibers so that they will not wash off.

SPRAY PAINTS Very effective stencil work can be carried out using enamel spray paints of the type available for touching up the finish on an automobile. However, applying these paints requires a practiced hand, and you must experiment thoroughly first. A wide range of colors is available, and very soft, delicate effects can be achieved. You can get similar results using thinned japan colors and a spray gun, but again you must be well acquainted with the technique before undertaking such a project. The paint must be sprayed very lightly or it will drip under the stencil.

TURPENTINE You will need turpentine for thinning japan colors and for cleaning brushes and stencils. Keep a generous supply on hand while you are stencilling.

PAINT THINNER Paint thinner, or mineral spirits, can be used for cleaning brushes and stencils. You may prefer it for thinning japan paint because it is less toxic than turpentine.

GLASS PALETTE OR PLATES Mix your paints on old plates and saucers or on a glass palette. If you are mixing several colors as you work, a glass sheet makes a good palette on which you can arrange individual areas of color.

COOKIE SHEET A cookie sheet or metal tray is an ideal base from which to work. On it you can arrange stacks of paper towels, dishes of paint, pots of turpentine, teaspoons and palette knives, and your brushes. With all your equipment collected together in this way, you can move your base around with you as you work.

PALETTE KNIFE Use an artists' palette knife for thinning and mixing paint evenly.

OLD JARS AND COFFEE CANS Small glass jars are useful for mixing and storing larger quantities of paint when you want to keep the mix consistent. If you are storing paint in them for later use during a project, seal them with plastic film and a lid. Coffee tins are good containers for rinsing brushes.

ALUMINUM FOIL OR PLASTIC WRAP When you pause in your stencilling either for a short break or overnight, you can prevent your brushes from drying out by wrapping and sealing them tightly in aluminum foil or plastic wrap.

MASKING TAPE Masking tape is used for holding stencils in place on the surface to be stencilled. Replace it when it fails to stick adequately. It can also be used to mask off unwanted areas of a stencil temporarily.

FOR FINISHING OFF

The way in which you finish your stencilled surface is usually a question of preference and depends to a great extent on the project. *Warning:* Do not use lacquer-type varnishes over japan colors.

POLYURETHANE VARNISH Today polyurethane varnish is most commonly used for finishing projects, particularly those painted on wooden surfaces. Gloss, semi-gloss, and matte varnishes are available. They can either be applied straight from the can or "cut" with a small proportion of solvent to make a lighter coat.

Techniques

As with any craft, you will, in time, develop your own methods of stencilling, finding shortcuts and procedures that suit your way of working. But for the beginner there are a few dos and don'ts and other useful tips that will make stencilling much easier and hence more enjoyable. In this book you are presented with projects by eight different designers, who will share with you the special techniques and knowhow that they have developed over the years. But there

is a basic method from which all their stencilling derives, and we recommend you read and understand it thoroughly before embarking on any of the projects. Within the individual projects we will discuss particular techniques relevant to them, some of which can also be applied to other forms of stencilling.

TRANSFERRING A STENCIL OUTLINE

The patterns for your stencils can come from an infinite number of sources, which are discussed in greater depth in Chapter 2. Once you have found a design you want to use, you need to extract it from its source, perhaps enlarge or reduce it, and copy it onto stencil material.

In this book all the stencil outlines are given for individual projects. Some need enlarging, but in all instances the outlines can be either traced or photocopied from the page and used without any further interpretation.

Tracing a Design

This is a simple process. Lay a piece of tracing paper flat over the design and anchor it with masking tape to prevent it from moving as you draw. Then with a sharp soft pencil, carefully trace the outlines. When two stencil outlines are shown superimposed, you can either trace the entire design as it appears on the page and separate the outlines as you draw your stencils on acetate, or you can separate them at this stage, tracing only the outlines for one color on one piece of paper and those for the next color on another piece of paper, and so forth. It is not recommended that you trace your design directly from the book onto your acetate, as it is difficult to get the book to lie flat and distortions will occur.

Scaling a Pattern Up or Down

Scaling a design up or down can be done either before or after you trace your outline from its source. Photostatting is a very simple means of having a pattern accurately enlarged or reduced to the required size, directly from the book

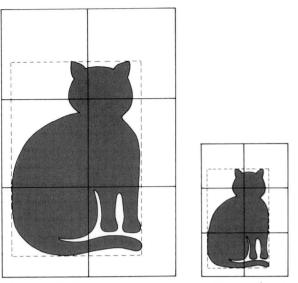

Figure 1 Enlarging or reducing a pattern using a grid. After working out the size of the larger or smaller grid, draw in each new square exactly the same outline that appears in the original.

or a tracing. Either consult the project instructions for the number of times the outline must be increased or decreased or work it out with a ruler to correspond with the final size you want. Try to work in units of the design. For instance, if the given size of a design is 5 inches wide and 8 inches high and your space is 8 inches by 12½ inches, you will find it best to enlarge the design 1½ times to give you an outline 7½ inches by 12 inches. Indicate how much you want your outline enlarged or reduced, and the photostat house will process it accordingly.

You can also use 1-inch-grid graph paper to enlarge or reduce a pattern. First you must trace the outline onto a clean piece of tracing paper. Then draw a square or rectangle around the outline so that each side of the rectangle just touches the outermost point of the design. Make sure your corners form right angles by using a T-square or right angle. Then divide the rectangle into ½- or 1-inch squares, depending on the size of the design, starting at the middle and working out evenly to either side.

Work out the extent of the enlargement or reduction you desire. If the outline has been divided into 1-inch squares and is to be enlarged

1½ times, mark off a rectangle on the graph paper consisting of the same number of squares but with the squares falling on every 1½ inches. Starting at the center, copy the pattern in the corresponding squares on the graph paper, drawing in each new square exactly the same outlines that appear in the original, so that the outermost points of the new outline just touch the perimeters of the new rectangle. Draw first in pencil so that you can erase mistakes, and then go over the finished outline in marker pen. You can reduce an outline in the same way using a smaller grid to correspond with the reduction required.

TRANSFERRING THE OUTLINE ONTO STENCIL MATERIAL

The instructions that follow are intended for acetate or Mylar® stencils, although the basic cutting techniques apply to all types of materials. Cutting waxed paper stencils from a stencil key is explained fully in Chapter 4.

Cut a piece of stencil material large enough to cover the stencil outline and leave at least 2 extra inches all around. This border is needed to accommodate the overlap of brushstrokes as you apply paint through the openings in the stencil. Otherwise the brushstrokes can smudge onto the surface you are stencilling. Place the stencil outline flat on a drawing board, holding it in position with masking tape. Then place the piece of stencil material on top of it. If you are using acetate, place it so that the side that curls away from you is face up. Flatten it completely and hold it in place over the tracing paper with masking tape.

The technique of stencilling is based on the idea of splitting up a design into its different areas of color so that one stencil is used for one color. Occasionally, if two separate colors appear sufficiently far apart, you can cut the outlines for two colors on one piece of stencil material and mask out the second color area as you stencil in the first color.

A stencil is composed of bridges that prevent the stencil material from collapsing as you

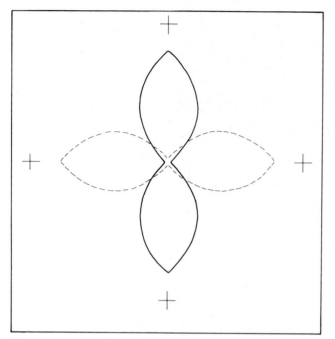

Figure 2 Examples of two kinds of registration marks. The broken outlines are registered on corresponding parts of the pattern, and the small crosses at the sides are for vertical and horizontal alignment.

cut out your design. More will be said about incorporating bridges in your designs in Chapter 2. It is important that, wherever a bridge is included in a design, you respect it and cut around it. It is also important to include registration marks on each stencil so that you can see as you work how one part of a design relates to the outline as a whole and can make sure that each part lines up accurately in the overall pattern. Registration marks can either be partial outlines of other elements in the design or exact vertical and horizontal rules for aligning the stencil.

Using a fine-nibbed technical drawing pen or permanent marker pen, trace the outlines for one color onto the acetate with a solid line.

If your stencil is composed of superimposed patterns, it is a good idea to trace the outlines of the other colors using a broken line, which you can use for registration. If you have included small registration marks for vertical and horizontal alignment, duplicate them onto the acetate with the aid of a ruler. Number the sten-

cil at the top right-hand corner according to the order in which it will be used. The number also helps to identify the correct side from which the stencil should be printed. Repeat this process for all the other stencils required for your particular project.

CUTTING THE STENCILS

Once you have drawn all the stencil outlines on separate pieces of acetate and numbered each stencil, you are ready to start cutting. Give yourself plenty of room; you will be turning the stencil and using your elbow and wrist considerably, and cramped working conditions will result in a badly cut stencil. Put a fresh blade in your utility knife, and place your glass or self-healing cutting mat on the work surface. Then lay your stencil drawing on the cutting mat.

You should cut a few stencils as practice until you have mastered the technique. Holding the knife firmly as if you were drawing with it, start cutting anywhere on a stencil outline. Cut directly on the line and not to either side. *Always cut toward you.* Use a continuous motion to avoid ragged edges, lifting the knife from the acetate as little as possible. Use your other hand to steady the piece of acetate. When you are cutting curves and circles, continue to cut toward yourself and turn the acetate with your hand to follow the bend of the curve. This is difficult to master at first, but don't become discouraged. Any stencil cutting is tiring to a beginner.

If your knife slips and you overcut, you can usually patch the area with transparent tape. Apply tape over the damaged spot on both sides of the stencil and then cut the tape to follow the cut edge of the stencil. If you have broken a bridge in the stencil, the damage may be more severe and a repair with tape may not hold. It is probably better to abandon that stencil and start again. Cutting straight lines in a stencil is sometimes made easier by a metal ruler, but take care to connect them gently with any continuing curves and do not cut beyond the length of the straight line indicated.

Your first few stencils will not be your best,

Cutting out the stencil openings in the acetate using a utility knife. *Photo by David Arky.*

but don't despair. Practice, and when you have a good stencil, you are ready to start experimenting with actually using it. Cut all your stencils at the beginning of a project and not as you go along.

PLANNING THE DISTRIBUTION

The next stage in creating your stencilled project involves accurately measuring and marking out the surface so that you know how many stencils will fit in the area, what size they should be, and just where they should be placed. You will have estimated this to some extent when initially deciding on the size of the stencil, but before you start to paint, you need to measure the surface so that you know your stencils will be evenly distributed and straight. Instructions

for positioning stencils are also given in the individual projects where a specific stencil has been designed for a particular surface. Depending on the surface and the design, there are several ways of positioning a stencilled pattern.

Using a Proof of the Stencil Outline

Once you have cut your stencil, it is a good idea to make a rough proof of the design on a piece of white paper. You can then stick this proof onto your surface with masking tape to get an idea of how the stencil will look. Several of these proofs can be used to establish an approximate balance in an arrangement. The height of a design being used on a wall, the distribution of a design being used on a floor, the depth of a design being used as a border—all can be successfully ascertained by this means.

Positioning Designs by Eye

Once you have juggled around with your proof, you can stencil using only your eye as a guide, without meticulous measuring. This is easier to do if you are stencilling a small flat area in front of you, such as the top of a chest or a piece of wrapping paper. A simple border consisting of a single small, repeating pattern can also be applied without measuring, provided that the edge of the stencil is sufficiently straight to act as an accurate guide. However, stencilling at random over a large surface, such as a wall, can pose problems for an unskilled stenciller. It is difficult to achieve a good balance when you are working close to a large surface and cannot see the overall effect easily.

Measuring and Marking

How you mark out your surface will depend on the project and the way you will be working. If you are applying a border around an area, then you need an accurate measurement of how far in, or down, the border should be placed all the way around, and little else. If the border pattern is one that needs centering, then you also have to mark the center of each run of the border so that you can work evenly to either side.

If, however, you are working over an entire area on a piece of furniture, the lid of a box, a floor, or a wall, then an even distribution of the design is usually required. With the exception of the wall, this is done by finding the exact center of the area and working outward from there. In the case of the wall, you will be working downward, from top to bottom, rather than radiating out from a central point.

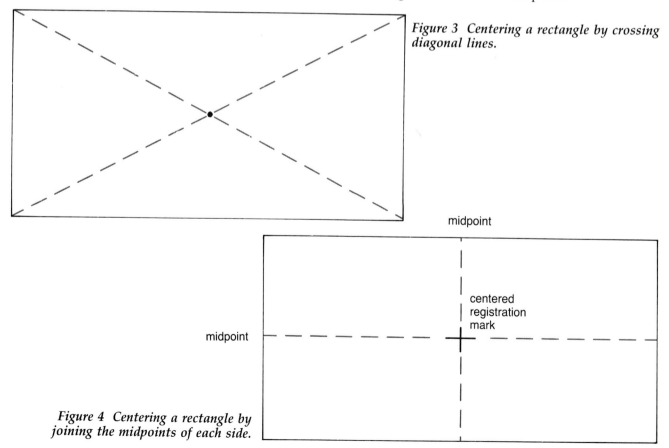

Figure 3 Centering a rectangle by crossing diagonal lines.

midpoint

midpoint

centered
registration
mark

Figure 4 Centering a rectangle by joining the midpoints of each side.

CENTERING A SMALL RECTANGLE The lid of a box, the top of a chest or table, a floorcloth, a card, and a piece of paper are all centered in this way. Before you start, make sure that all corners form right angles if possible. You can find the center of the rectangle most easily by drawing diagonal crossing lines from corner to corner (see fig. 3). Or you can find the midpoint of each side and join the lines so that they cross (see fig. 4). In both instances the point where the lines intersect is the exact center, but in the latter method you can draw a registration mark at the center which can be used to align the stencils.

CENTERING A CIRCLE The lid of a round box, a circular tabletop, and a circular floorcloth can all be centered in this way. If the circular object is small enough, you can trace around the perimeter onto a piece of paper, cut out the circle, and fold it in half. Then fold the half circle in half to divide the circle into quarters. The point where the fold lines cross is the center, which can then be transferred onto the original object. Or you can use a tape measure or ruler to measure the widest part of the circle (the diameter) and draw a faint chalk or pencil line across. Working at right angles to this line, find the diameter in the opposite direction and mark the line. The

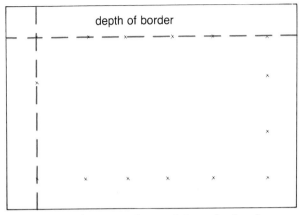

Figure 5 Marking out the position of a border stencil

point where the lines intersect is the center.

POSITIONING A BORDER DESIGN Borders can be placed around almost any surface, from a greeting card to a door frame. Whether your pattern is a simple, continuously repeating outline or a more complex motif, you need to mark on the surface just how far in, or down, it will be applied. To do this, use a ruler to measure accurately in from the edge at several points along the edge, marking these points with a dash in chalk or pencil (see fig. 5). Using a straightedge, you can join the points together if necessary to give a continuous registration mark on the sur-

Registering and positioning a stencil for a border on the wall surface. The registration line on the stencil corresponds with pencil ticks on the wall surface. The last stencil opening on the left is registered over the last print on the wall. *Photo by David Arky.*

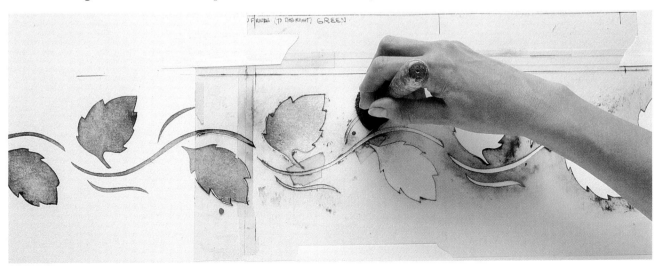

face. The dashes or line should correspond to an equivalent registration line on the stencil so that you can align the stencil accurately on the surface.

Just how you align your stencil is a matter of choice. You can draw a line directly underneath your stencil openings so that the pattern prints just above these points, or you can draw your registration line an inch below or above the stencil openings so that the stencil prints above or below this line. Include a registration outline, marked with a broken line at each end of a simple repeating border motif, so that you can register the design on previously stencilled outlines (see photograph on page 23).

CENTERING A BORDER DESIGN One of the first problems encountered by the novice stenciller is how to make a design fit evenly within an allocated space. This is particularly important when you are working with a border that includes a bold motif, such as a swag. If you start at one end and work your way along, you can be left with a partial swag at the end. There are several ways to avoid this.

Always begin by measuring the length of the area in which the border must fit. Then find the center and mark it. You can now place the border unit over this point so that the center of the unit corresponds with the center of the length of the wall (or whatever surface you are stencilling) and work evenly to either side until you reach the ends. Or, if this leaves you with two partial prints at each end, you can place a motif on each side of the center point so that the prints at the ends are complete (see fig. 6). You should experiment with these possibilities on paper first before beginning to stencil.

If neither of these methods works, you may need to introduce more space between the units of the border, if you want the border to finish with a complete print at each end. Work this out on paper first, measuring the width of the stencil unit and dividing the length of the wall (or other surface) by this number. Then adjust the spacing accordingly.

Marking Out an Overall Pattern

When you are stencilling a floor, a wall, the top of a large piece of furniture, or a floorcloth with an exact (as opposed to randomly placed) pattern, it is necessary to mark off the surface first into equal units so that the pattern balances. If the area to be stencilled is large, such as a floor or a wall, you will need to use a plumb line and chalk box, which is described in the next section of this chapter; if it is sufficiently manageable,

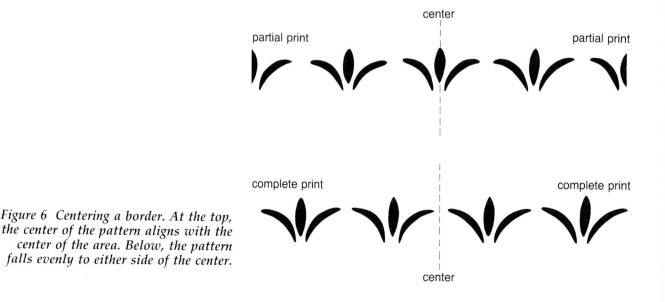

Figure 6 Centering a border. At the top, the center of the pattern aligns with the center of the area. Below, the pattern falls evenly to either side of the center.

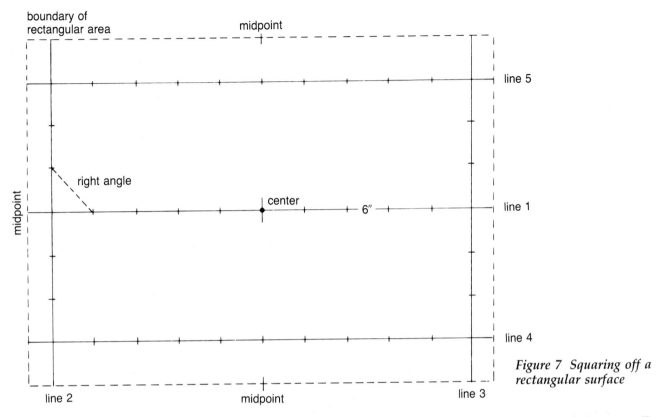

Figure 7 Squaring off a rectangular surface

you can use a tape measure and ruler and chalk or soft-lead pencil.

First, find and mark the center of the area by joining the mid-points on opposite sides of the rectangle. Next, draw a pencil line or snap a chalk line between the center points on two opposite sides of the rectangle (fig. 7, line 1). Decide what size the squares should be according to the size of your stencil pattern. If, for example, your stencil motif occupies a 5-inch square and requires a 1-inch border all round, you will need units of 6 inches. Starting at the center, mark points 6 inches apart along the line until you reach both ends. Then move to one end, and at the last point marked on the line, measure an *exact* right angle. Using this as your guide, draw a line crossing the first one and reaching the edges (line 2). When it is drawn, check that the intersection is perpendicular. Starting at the center, mark off this line in units of 6 inches in the same way.

This arrangement will now work like a T-square for marking off the rest of the area. For complete accuracy it is advisable to draw a similar perpendicular line at the other end of the original center line (line 3). Then join the two remaining sides of the rectangle, and mark each of the four sides off into 6-inch units. Finally, mark off the area in designated blocks, joining the points so that the entire area is squared off.

Using a Plumb Line

To square off a floor or mark a wall accurately, you need to use a plumb line and chalk box. Operating a plumb line requires two people, and for very large areas sometimes a third person to do the actual snapping. A plumb line is used to lay the line grid down on a floor or to find and mark the exact vertical of a wall.

FLOORS When you have marked out the measured points on a floor with pencil or chalk dots, you will use the plumb line to mark out the actual grid. One person stands at one end and holds the chalk box steady. The other per-

Using a plumb line to establish the true vertical on a wall.

Snapping the chalk line. *Photos by David Arky.*

son takes the end of the string and gently pulls it out from the box until the string reaches across the expanse to be marked. As the string is pulled out, the person holding the chalk box should hold a tissue under it to catch excess chalk dust. Once the plumb line extends between the two points, pull it tight and hold it just above the floor. Then gently lower it onto the floor, holding it firmly with a finger at either end and still stretching it tightly. One person should then gently and swiftly pluck the line so that it leaves a clearly defined chalk line on the surface. Rewind the string back into the box to freshen the chalk, and repeat the process.

Trial and error will tell you how much chalk you need; the line should be visible but not too heavy. Use white chalk dust on a dark surface and mix blue chalk dust with the white to mark a pale surface. The chalk lines can be removed with a clean rag. If traces remain, remove them with a clean kneaded eraser. Photographs showing the use of a plumb line to mark a floor appear in Chapter 10.

WALLS The same method of stretching and plucking the chalk line is used for marking walls. However, here the plumb line is also used to establish true vertical lines on the wall surface. One person stands on a stool or a stepladder and holds the entire line and chalk box at the point where the line needs to be registered. Holding the end of the string firmly, this person allows the box to drop gently until it reaches a point just above the floor. It must be allowed to hang freely. When the line has steadied itself and hangs still, the second person should press it with a finger against the wall and then snap it in the same way as for the floor. Only make chalk lines where your pattern will be dropping vertically on the wall. In this way you establish the true vertical line of the wall. In many houses the corners are not a satisfactory indication of the true vertical.

APPLYING THE STENCILS

When the surface is all mapped out and the positions and sequence of the stencils are clearly established, you are ready to start applying the paint. Stencilling is an easy process if you use the correct consistency of paint and the correct amount of paint on your brush. Before you start any project, you should practice applying paint through the stencil onto paper until you get a good proof. Once you have mastered this, you will find ways to add your own personal touches, such as shading, blending colors, varying the strength of colors, and so forth. At first, however, concentrate on controlling the paint and achieving a clearly defined print.

Setting Up a Stencilling Unit

First of all, set up a unit from which you can work. A cookie sheet or a tin tray makes a good base on which to arrange your materials. Line it with several thicknesses of newspapers. On this place a stack of paper towels, a stencilling brush, a small dish of turpentine and a teaspoon, a palette knife, a dish or saucer with your paint, and masking tape. This is your basic "kit," which you will need each time you stencil. Keep it all on the tray so that it is neat and tidy and can be moved around if necessary. Replace brushes and paint dishes as you introduce new colors and change paper towels frequently.

When you are working on a wall or a high border, you will need to work from a stepladder or a stool. In this situation keep your tray of materials and your stencils on a cart or small table that you can move around the room with you as you work. To save hopping up and down your ladder, wear an apron or overalls with a large pocket in the front so that you can keep a ruler, pencil, eraser, spare brushes, and paper towels close at hand. The same applies when you are stencilling a floor or a piece of furniture or even a large floorcloth or piece of fabric. Save time and energy by having a mobile unit on which you can store your equipment and keep it handy as you progress with your project.

Mixing the Paint

When you buy your paint, you will most probably know what colors you want to use. You may decide to use ready-mixed paint colors or you may want to mix a particular color. If you are using japan color in a manufactured shade, then all you need to do is to transfer a small quantity of the paint (about a teaspoonful) into a saucer and carefully add a few drops of turpentine. Stir the paint with a palette knife, adding enough turpentine to thin it to the consistency of heavy cream—no thinner. Be careful not to thin the paint too much or it will drip under the edges of the stencil.

If you are mixing two or more japan colors, add the tinting color in tiny amounts to the base color (see Chapter 2 for information about color mixing) and thin the paint at the same time with a few drops of turpentine. Stencilling requires very small amounts of paint—at the most usually a few tablespoonsful—so mix enough to complete the job but try not to overestimate and waste your paints. It is a good idea to make a record of a mixed color on an index card, by painting a swatch and listing the proportions of colors, in case you need to mix more.

Japan colors will dry out as they stand uncovered. If you are not using all the paint at once, keep it in a small sealed can or jar, and add drops of turpentine to the paint in your saucer if it starts to dull and become thick as you work. If you are using acrylic paints, they may be used directly from the tube without thinning. If they begin to dry, mix them with drops of *water* (not turpentine) to recover the correct consistency.

Applying the Paint

Until you have watched someone stencil, you won't understand what small quantities of paint are required to achieve a successful print. Print your first stencil on sturdy plain paper. Position the stencil and secure it with masking tape. Dip a dry, clean brush into the paint. Then, using a circular motion, work the paint into the bristles on dry paper towels to remove the excess and distribute the paint evenly among the bristles.

Then gently apply the paint through the stencil openings in a circular motion, flexing the bristles and working toward the edges. Pouncing, stroking, and squashing the bristles will all result in disaster. Just gently and evenly distribute the paint. You can also use a stippling technique, dabbing on the paint in a straight up-and-down motion until you achieve the coverage you want. It should not be necessary to refill your brush with paint for one stencil.

When you think you have completed your first print, stand back and look at it, lifting the stencil away from the paper. If paint has dripped under the stencil, you need a thicker consistency and less paint on the brush. If it is too faint, you need more paint and perhaps a slightly thinner consistency. If it is adequately colored but looks flat and uninteresting, try shading the paint within the stencil. The stencil outlines should be crisp, perhaps with a very delicate edge visible where paint has collected against the edge of the stencil. Remember, too, that the paint may become slightly lighter as it dries.

Always use a clean brush when you start working with a new color; do not be tempted to rinse the one you are working with and continue with it. It is also a good idea to have a fresh saucer to hold the new color of paint, and fresh paper towels are essential.

If paint collects in your brush as you are working, making the bristles lose their flexibility and feel heavy, work out the paint on a pad of paper towels dampened with turpentine and wipe off the excess paint around the head of the brush. *Never immerse your brush in turpentine in the middle of a project.* You will not be able to get rid of the turpentine, which can ruin your efforts to stencil. If paint has built up around the stencil openings, you can clean it off with a paper towel moistened with turpentine.

Coping with Mistakes

Most stencilling mistakes can be corrected. The beginner's fear of having to repaint a recently painted wall or resand a floor is usually unfounded. Small smudges and tiny drips can be eradicated with a kneaded eraser. It may be better to let the paint dry very slightly before correcting with an eraser because very wet paint will smudge even more. A drip can be caught with a cotton swab or tissue lightly moistened with turpentine, and the resulting paint stain removed with an eraser. If the paint has run under the stencil opening, again use a cotton swab or tissue to blot it up. Make sure there is no wet paint on the back side of the stencil before you continue. Also, always keep a small can of your background paint and a fine brush handy so you can touch up resistant smudges.

Fingerprints are one of the biggest hazards of stencilling. It is easy to collect paint on your fingers and to leave fingerprints on the surface as you move your stencils. Try to work cleanly.

If you actually put part of the design in the wrong place and cannot correct your mistake by any of the above methods, take a cloth or a paper towel soaked in turpentine and rub out the entire element. If a smudge remains, try wiping it out again with turpentine and, if necessary, touch up the area with your extra background paint. Do not try to reapply the stencil until this new coat of paint is completely dry.

Remember, usually no mistake is so disastrous that it cannot be corrected. Stencilling is an artistic craft, and as such it gives you license

Working the paint out of the brush before applying it. A pad of paper towels for this purpose is placed on a tray, along with a dish of paint, a palette knife, paint solvent, a teaspoon, and the stencil brush. This arrangement makes a convenient unit from which to stencil. *Photo by David Arky.*

From left to right: Wet, dry, and perfect prints. When the paint is too wet, it runs under the stencil and results in badly defined edges and a blotchy print. When it is too dry, the print is faint and shading is difficult. A perfect print should be delicately shaded, with crisp edges, and the separate stencils evenly registered. *Photo by David Arky.*

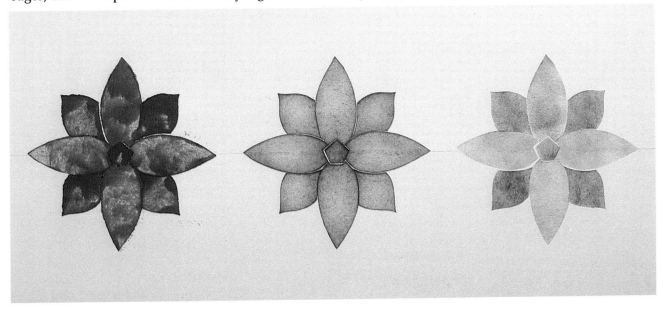

to improvise, change your design slightly if necessary, add extra elements—and sometimes the improvisations will be an improvement!

Acrylic Paints

All these instructions for applying and correcting japan colors hold true for acrylic paints as well. Remember, however, that the solvent for acrylic paint is *water*, not turpentine. Also, when acrylic paint dries, it forms a skin that can be difficult to erase, so mistakes must be corrected promptly.

In the projects in Chapter 4 the acrylic paint is applied so that it forms a thick, opaque surface on the boxes rather than a delicate, almost translucent effect. This is a matter of choice, but you will not achieve the same depth and lucidity with acrylic paint that you can with japan color.

FINISHING OFF WITH VARNISH

With the exception of walls, stencilled surfaces usually require some kind of seal to protect them. A varnish is usually used and can be either sprayed on small objects or applied with a brush on larger projects. Today the most commonly used sealant is a polyurethane varnish, which is available from hardware stores in cans and from art-supply stores in smaller aerosol containers. Remember that varnish will deepen colors underneath somewhat and may cast a yellowish hue over white or pale colors.

Polyurethane varnish is available in three finishes: gloss, semi-gloss or satin, and matte or flat. The gloss finish produces a brilliant, clear coating that seems artificially shiny. You would use this only if you wanted an almost lacquer-like surface on solid colors. The effect is rich and adds depth to the stencilled colors underneath. The semi-gloss or satin varnish gives a silky sheen to the surface, like the sheen of a naturally polished surface. It is ideal for stencilled wooden floors and furniture where a sheen enhances the design. Matte or flat varnish has no shine at all and leaves the surface looking unfinished. It is ideal for natural wood projects where you do not want a polished effect, or for painted wooden

furniture where you want the handiwork to stand out and not be screened by a glossy coating.

You should apply at least two coats of varnish to a finished item, but first make sure the stencilling is completely dry by testing a small area. Apply the varnish with a flat paintbrush about 1 to 2 inches wide, depending on the scale of the project. Wipe the surface with a tack cloth between applications, and make sure the first coat of varnish has dried before you apply a second; this may take from one to three days. The varnish can be diluted with solvent to make a thinner coat if you wish.

If you choose to use spray varnish, follow the instructions on the can and use a mask to avoid inhaling the fine spray. Always work near an open window when you are using toxic aerosol substances. Again, you will need two coats of spray varnish for a durable finish.

A varnished surface can be lightly sponged with warm water and mild detergent to clean it.

Bleeding

You should be aware of the possibility of paint "bleeding" when you apply varnish. Some varnishes can cause certain pigments, especially reds, to run. If this occurs, stop applying the varnish and apply a coat of shellac or spray varnish over the susceptible areas. Allow this to dry thoroughly, then continue with the varnishing.

CLEANING UP

You will not enjoy your next attempt at stencilling if your brushes are clogged and the rest of your equipment is dirty. You should clean up even if you are just pausing for the night. If you have been stencilling with japan colors, turpentine or mineral spirits will be your solvent. If you have been using acrylics, you can simply clean up with soap and water.

If you intend to use your brushes again the next day, you do not have to clean them completely. Instead, you can work out as much paint as possible on paper towels and then wrap and seal the brushes tightly in foil or plastic wrap so that they will not dry out. Leave them in a cool place overnight.

When you have finished using a japan color, rinse the brush thoroughly in turpentine or mineral spirits. Pour about an inch of spirits into two or three jars and rinse the brush consecutively in each bath, leaving it to soak for an hour or more in the first one. Squeeze out the excess spirits with a paper towel and then shampoo the brush with mild detergent, cleaning up into its center. Rinse the bristles thoroughly and shake out the excess water. You should allow brushes to dry naturally, preferably with the bristles pointing downward. You can suspend them by the handles or rest them on paper towels.

To clean your stencils, cover a table with several layers of newspaper. Remove and throw away all the pieces of masking tape from the stencils. Remember that stencils are delicate, and it is in cleaning that damage can often occur. Make a bed of paper towels on the newspaper and place a stencil flat on it, painted side up. Moisten a couple of tissues with turpentine and gently rub the surface of the stencil to remove the paint. Work gently and from the outer edges in. Do not rub harshly in the center cut-out portion or you will tear the stencil. When one side is clean, turn the stencil over and repeat the process.

Use the spirits left over from cleaning the brushes to wash out saucers and other equipment. If dried-on paint is very resistant, try a pot scrubber or steel wool to lift it.

STORING YOUR MATERIALS

It pays to take good care of your equipment because it will last longer. Always store your materials neatly where they will not get harmed. Stencils, in particular, are susceptible to damage, and brushes can quickly become ruined if left lying around. Keep your stencilling equipment in a tool or tackle box or in an allocated drawer, and store your stencils flat, preferably in an artists' portfolio case or a special drawer. Stack the stencils with sheets of paper between them for greater protection. Make sure paint cans are tightly sealed and stored right side up. When a project is finished, it does not mean your stencils and paints are also finished. Keep them clean and ready for your next project.

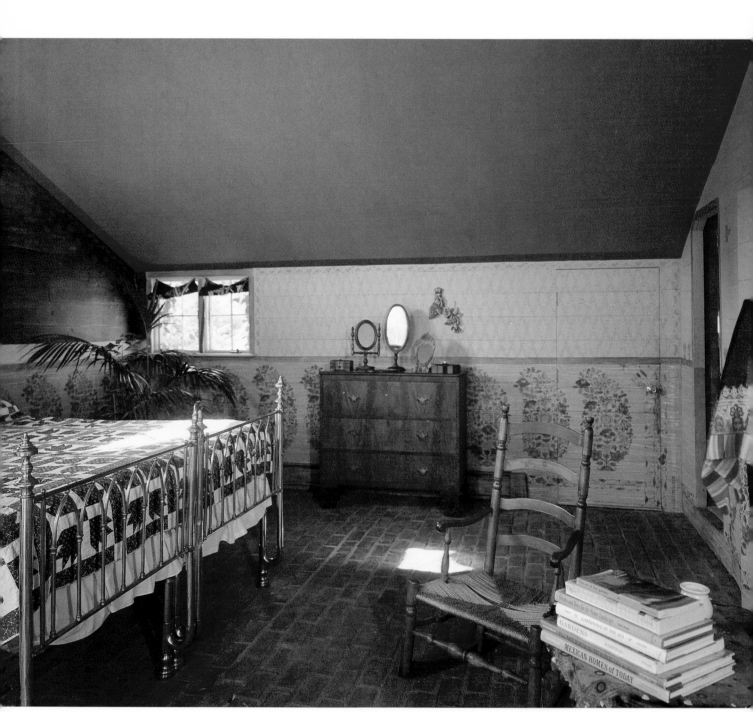

An imaginative use of color and large paisley wall stencils executed by Cile Lord transform this room in designer Gina Beadle's converted barn in Amagansett, New York. Notice how the border stripes and motifs give the room unity. *Photo by Hans Namuth.*

Opposite page: A master of *trompe l'oeil* effects, Jeff Greene stencilled this "skylight" on a ceiling in Bergdorf Goodman's, New York. *Photo © Evergreene Studios.*

CHAPTER TWO
Color & Design

Most of us are aware of what pleases and what displeases our eyes. We know what shapes and patterns we like and what color combinations we enjoy. Left on our own to translate these shapes and colors into actual two-dimensional forms and patterns, we flounder, lacking the artistic skill to interpret what we appreciate in our mind's eye. A stencil, however, can give us the means to create our own designs. It provides us with a fool-proof record of a shape and color, which we can then try out in different configurations and distributions to find a pattern that pleases us. Because stencilling does not require skilled draftsmanship, it offers all of us the opportunity to discover the satisfaction of creating a design of our own.

A stencil has numerous design possibilities. With just one outline and one color, you can learn to appreciate how a pattern fits together. Begin by cutting a stencil from the outline given on page 35. Use it to make a number of prints on plain white paper, flopping the stencil occasionally (turning it over and printing it) so that the outlines bend in both directions. Cut out each outline, close to the print, and then rule a piece of rough white paper (approximately 20 inches

by 28 inches) into a grid of 3-inch squares. Using this grid as a distribution guide, you can experiment with creating a pattern and see the ways in which different arrangements produce different effects.

Take the cut-out proofs and play with them on the piece of paper, using the squares as a guide for positioning, until you find a configuration that pleases you. Experiment with border arrangements and allover configurations. Always stand back to look at your arrangements, and you will find that a pattern changes dramatically in its effect when viewed close up and from a distance. When you first start to arrange the proof pieces, you will probably place them right side up and aligned with the grid. Try also turning them upside down and on their sides in both directions; juxtapose shapes that bend in opposite directions.

Even if you do not hit upon a particularly satisfactory arrangement at first, you will discover that one stencil can be used to create many completely original patterns. You will also discover instances where a single stencil appears inadequate, where a bordering stripe or a different element could greatly enhance the design.

By experimenting, you can teach yourself about the elements necessary to a pleasing pattern, which is the foundation of creative stencilling.

Stencilling entails the repetitive application of an outline or collection of outlines within a given area. As you might expect, if the motif is rigid and is applied uniformly across the surface, the result may look static and pedantic. Whether a static or dynamic pattern is preferred is, of course, a matter of taste, but generally a more appealing effect is obtained when movement is introduced within a pattern. Movement is synonymous with interest; it implies that the eye is led in a variety of directions within the pattern, so that all aspects of the space are visually explored.

A further advantage of introducing movement within a design is that it makes the pattern more versatile. A curving tendril or stem can be led around a corner, shaped around an arch, or fitted within a given space without an obvious imbalance in pattern.

Achieving Movement in a Pattern

Movement within a pattern can be created in a number of ways. Initially it depends on the motifs you choose to make up your pattern. More will be said about sources for designs and motifs later in this chapter, but basically there are two types of outlines: those which are symmetrical, self-contained units occupying a uniform space, and those which are asymmetrical, curved and extending outward in a variety of directions and consequently leading the eye in a variety of directions. Usually it is best to have a mixture of both, but by including asymmetrical elements you will be able to achieve movement in your pattern.

To understand this, consider arranging a bunch of flowers. Imagine that you have a straight-sided vase that lends nothing to the shape of the stems of the flowers. If all the stems are rigid and straight, you will only be able to arrange the flowers so that they stand straight up. The arrangement will be uninteresting. If, how-

ever, in selecting your flowers, you are able to choose stems that bend first one way and then another, that spread to one side, then in front, then to the other side, you can create an arrangement that not only sympathizes with the bend in the stems but is full and pleasing to the eye. These principles of composition apply in exactly the same way to stencilling. Of course, this does not mean that all stencil outlines must be floral, but it illustrates the difference that natural curves and shapes can make in achieving a balanced and interesting composition.

Once your design incorporates even the most rudimentary movement, perhaps two outwardly curving lines, a space is opened up for more elements in the pattern. For example, you could place an element in the middle of two curving outlines to fill the space created by them. Or each curving line could lead toward an element or group of elements. A combination of asymmetrical and symmetrical elements within a design can, in fact, serve to exaggerate the movement in the pattern and establish a pace. Moreover, by introducing additional elements in this way, you begin to balance your design. When considering the possibilities, view your stencil as a tool. If you have a stencil that curves outward to the right, you need not make another identical stencil that curves out to the left. Remember that a stencil can be flopped to produce a mirror image of its original shape.

In an allover pattern, movement is introduced by staggering. That is, repeats are offset so that elements of a pattern do not lie in rigid, repetitious rows but hop from one position to another as the eye progresses across or down (see fig. 8).

Space Within a Pattern

Two important considerations will affect the amount of space you leave between units of your pattern. First you should decide on how much intervening space the units of your design require to be distinctive and yet connected. Then you will need to modify the amount of space

Figure 8 Experimenting with pattern

Begin with a simple tulip motif.

Flop it to create movement and interest in a border pattern. Combine it with other elements to form a more elaborate pattern.

Arrange it to provide movement within an allover pattern.

according to the size and shape of the area you are stencilling.

When an allover pattern is involved, as on a floor, spacing is particularly important. Once you have marked off the floor into a squared grid, you can either place one unit of the design in each square or you can alternate squares of pattern with blank squares. Alternating the pattern with blank space is effective if the design is particularly dense, but if the design already incorporates considerable space, you may find it more effective to cover the entire floor. If you decide to alternate squares of pattern with blank squares, you should consider including a border around the outside edge to anchor the design and give an outline where blank squares occur at the edges. Look at the way in which patchwork and appliquéd quilts have been constructed. Some of the most beautiful and most balanced spatial designs are to be found in the products of this folk craft.

In wall stencilling, the amount of space within the design is important if the overall pattern is to be reminiscent of wallpaper. More frequently, however, wall stencilling is used to enhance architectural details or to create a more compositional effect, and therefore the space in which the pattern will fit is of more consequence than the space within the pattern.

In most instances, the amount of space required within border stencil patterns is first determined by the dimensions of the design and then is modified for the area in which the border must fit. Generally, a border high up will need more space between each unit of the design than a border lower down, and a border with large motifs will require more intervening space than one with small motifs.

Sources for Stencil Designs

There is a wealth of sources from which you can derive inspiration for stencil designs, and the ones described here are only a start. Ideas for sources are also listed in each of the individual chapters.

FREEHAND DESIGNS Those of you who have a talent for drawing will be able to create any number of outlines for all manner of surfaces. But even those who do not feel particularly adept at drawing may discover that, in fact, drawing your own outlines is not so difficult after all. Drawing for stencils is really a matter of duplicating shapes. When you consider a possible object or form as a stencil outline, first reduce it in your mind's eye to a two-dimensional silhouette and make this silhouette the outline for your stencil. You can then break the outline down into the various areas of color that will correspond to the individual stencils required for that subject. Drawing from already drawn forms, so that you are copying rather than interpreting, can help you understand how an outline breaks down.

Geometric shapes, which are easier to draw, are often best executed by hand, where precise measuring pays off. Squares and triangles can be drawn with the aid of a ruler, while a compass will produce a perfect circle. Sawtooth and checkerboard patterns can be rendered easily by hand. Use graph paper as a guide for distributing your pattern evenly on a surface.

TEXTILES Printed and woven fabrics are an excellent source for stencil outlines and are particularly suitable because the patterns have already been translated into two-dimensional form. It is easy to trace an outline from fabric by stretching the fabric tightly over a drawing board or pin board of some sort and then laying tracing paper over it. The outlines of the fabric pattern can be lightly traced and then transferred into stencil outlines.

CERAMICS Patterned china and earthenware also offer a wide variety of two-dimensional designs, but the task of reproducing them may be more complicated. If the pattern appears on a flat plate or saucer, you may be able to trace it directly, but otherwise you will have to rely on your drawing skills to copy the design, which you can then scale up or down as necessary. Graph paper will help you achieve a more accurate rendering.

Quilts Appliquéd and patchwork quilts are one of the richest sources of stencil outlines. Not only are the patterns already two-dimensional, but they are in outline form. Again, it may be easier to redraw an outline rather than trying to trace it. You can also derive stencil patterns from books on patchwork and quilting, either from photographs of the finished quilts or from patterns for making the quilts.

Illustrated Books Books are an excellent source of design ideas. You can find inspiration in books on quilts, ceramics, textiles, wallpapers, furniture, floral and animal illustration, needlecraft, woodcraft, and architecture. Art books depicting stylistic trends from the earliest primitive art to contemporary art offer an almost limitless supply of designs that you can adapt for stencilling. Often libraries have photocopying machines, and you may find drawing an outline from a photocopy an easier task. Be careful to observe the rules of copyright, however. Many patterns reside in the public domain and can be copied without any problem. If a piece of work is still under copyright, however, you must not reproduce it for your own commercial benefit (that is, to sell as your own work) without first seeking permission from the copyright owner. This applies to all previously published designs, including those on fabrics and ceramics. So long as you are not using the patterns commercially, you will be safe, but always respect another person's work.

Architectural Elements A keen eye will soon discern the stencilling possibilities offered by various architectural forms of decoration. Dentils, cornices, picture rails, door frames, and other architectural ornaments can all be translated into stencil patterns. It may be difficult at first to work out ways of interpreting them because of their context and their three-dimensional form. If you have this problem, study them in photographs rather than in real life since the photograph reduces them to two dimensions.

Ethnic Art Japanese, Chinese, Indian, South American, Egyptian, Scandinavian, and European ethnic art all offer a wide and varied source of stencilling themes. In many instances the folk renderings of these cultures are expressed in simple two-dimensional forms so that extracting them for stencilling purposes is an easy matter. Postcards in museum shops can be a convenient means of obtaining examples of motifs and color combinations.

Translating a Motif into a Stencil

A motif or series of motifs being used as a stencil design must be broken down into a suitable form from which one or more stencils can be made. The most important part of translating an outline into a stencil is separating the outline into the stencil openings and the necessary interlinking bridges.

Bridges Bridges are the fine uncut areas of material in a stencil linking the various openings. They serve two purposes. First, they prevent the stencil from collapsing in the cut-out area. Second, they separate different colors within one element of a pattern. Therefore, the number of stencils needed for a given outline depends on the number of colors you want and the number of bridges required to hold the stencil.

Figure 9 This motif requires two separate stencils, one for the top of the design and one for the base. One or two colors may therefore be used.

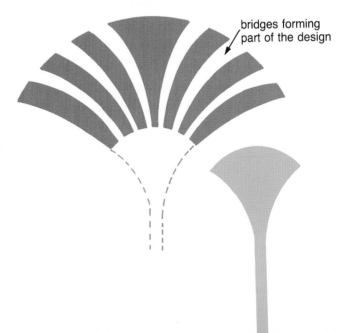

bridges forming
part of the design

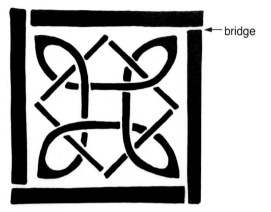

Figure 11 *Bridges in this border stripe prevent the stencil from collapsing. The stencil is moved over slightly after the first printing so that the square can be completed.*

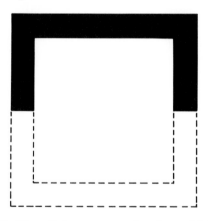

Figure 12 *Stencil for a square border, which must be printed twice to complete the square.*

Figure 10 *Two stencils are superimposed to eradicate the bridges, even though the stencil may be printed in one color.*

Bridges in a stencil can be concealed by subsequently overlaying other stencil forms and filling in the unpainted areas, or they can be used to separate the various parts of a motif. Usually, the more evident the bridge, the more two-dimensional the print. If you want no bridges to show, you may need to cut two stencils even when the complete motif is to be printed in one color (see fig. 10). To retain a continuous band within a stencil, such as a square border stripe, you will also need to employ bridges to prevent the center from dropping out (see fig. 11). You can also print the band as two halves, which are aligned end to end to make a continuous print (see fig. 12).

When you are considering a motif for a possible stencil outline, you must visualize how it will break down into separate colors and hence separate stencils. Different colors usually require different stencils, as do different shades. Where two colors appear sufficiently far apart in an outline, it is possible to accommodate them both within one stencil. Separating an outline into individual stencils is often difficult for an untrained eye to visualize. Practice by studying the various stencil outlines in this book and seeing how they have been broken down.

REGISTRATION MARKS When two or more stencils are cut for one outline, the second and subsequent stencils must have registration marks drawn on their surfaces. Registration marks are exact references to the other elements of the stencil that are printed before and afterward. They are usually marked on the acetate with a broken permanent line, and they indicate exactly the parts of the design with which that stencil must be lined up to complete the motif (see fig. 13).

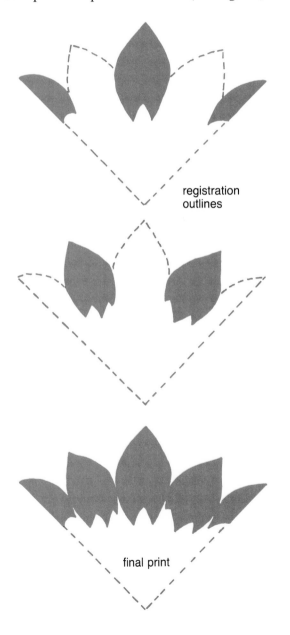

registration outlines

final print

Figure 13 Two stencils for one print prevent the outline from becoming continuous.

Color

The graphic impact of a stencilled design depends on how the parts are broken down to form a pattern, but equally important is the effect of color. Color brings the design alive, allowing you to give it your own personal touch and to tailor it to your own taste. As Josef Albers says in *Interaction of Color* (New Haven, Conn.: Yale University Press, rev. ed., 1975), "Good painting, good coloring, is comparable to good cooking. Even a good cooking recipe demands tasting and repeated tasting while it is being followed. And the best tasting still depends on a cook with taste."

There are two important considerations to keep in mind when selecting colors for stencilling. One is the way colors react when placed side by side, and the other is the effect created when one color is placed over another. The first relationship is concerned with the assembling of colors within a pattern, when colors are chosen for visual effect. The second relationship comes into play when these colors are laid over a background color. The effect of colors placed side by side is very different from the effect of colors placed one over another, and yet both must be considered when stencilling. No arrangement of colors will be successful without careful consideration of the background color and its effects on the stencil colors.

CHOOSING STENCIL COLORS

There are two ways to determine what colors to use in stencil patterns: Look at the colors in your room and use them as a source, or decide on the colors you want for the stencils and match the colors in your room to them. This will obviously depend on whether or not you want and can afford to redecorate your present furnishings. Whichever method you use, you must then think carefully about the way in which you will arrange the colors within your design. Stencilling becomes more realistic when the colors are arranged naturally. A broad palette of contrasting as well as coordinating colors is much closer to nature than a monotone selection. If you are seeking an effect reminiscent of freehand painting, you will achieve it by using a broad palette of colors; repeating monotones emphasize the stencilled form.

Contrast is important in a stencilled design to give it depth. Harmony is important to give it continuity and progression. Light and dark shades of a color will lend a more natural effect. Stencilling offers you the opportunity to introduce as much or as little contrasting color, tonal gradation, or shading as you want. When you are considering color combinations for your design, study existing patterns in fabrics, ceramics, or any of the design sources listed earlier in this chapter. Notice where contrasting colors were incorporated and to what extent, and borrow from the patterns that please you. Look at flowers and leaves in nature, and examine how the various colors interact and the breadth of colors that are present in what may seem at first to be one color.

Experiment with different color arrangements on paper, just as you experimented with design layouts. Because in stencilling the choice of colors is yours alone, you should take the time to explore all the possibilities of your palette. Once you have decided on your outlines and cut your stencils, mix a variety of colors to try out different effects. When you find color combinations that please you, make proofs of them on paper. Then cut out the proofs and stick them with masking tape to the surface to be stencilled. Stand back and examine the way in which they interact within the room. A color combination that seems effective close up might become lost when applied to a large surface and viewed from a distance.

In making your color decisions, you will need a good selection of paint colors to experiment with. When you first start to stencil, you may be content merely to follow the recipe for a project and copy the colors exactly. Much of the pleasure of stencilling, however, lies in the flexibility it offers you, in color as well as pattern. Once you feel confident that you will pursue stencilling seriously as a hobby, you should invest in as broad a range of colors as you can afford. Many subtle hues can be achieved by careful mixing, but there are some basic colors that give you the widest palette possible. The range of japan colors available will differ slightly with different manufacturers, but the ones listed below are common to most.

White	Flake white, striping white, or zinc white
Black	Lamp black
Blue	Ultramarine blue Permanent blue Prussian blue
Green	CP green dark CP green medium CP green light Emerald green
Red	Poster red Venetian red American red

Designed by Lynn Goodpasture.

Yellow   French yellow ochre
            Chrome yellow medium
            Chrome yellow light

Brown   Raw umber
            Burnt umber

Japan colors lack crimson and violet shades, and so you have to resort to mixing artists' oil colors such as alizarin crimson and cobalt violet with a japan color base to achieve these colors. Artists' oils are a useful alternative for tinting a japan color base, providing the proportion of oil paint to japan color does not exceed one part to four parts. Otherwise the oil paint will impair the drying properties of the japan colors.

Artists' oil paints can take the place of some shades of japan color and can provide a concentrated burst of color to a japan color base. Useful colors of oil paint to have are:

Permanent green deep
Permanent green medium
Winsor green
Cobalt blue
Ultramarine blue
Manganese blue
Naples yellow
Cadmium yellow medium
Cadmium yellow light
Cadmium red light
Burnt umber

MIXING COLORS

Always bear in mind the small quantities of paint that are required to tint a color. Whatever your craft, it is usually best to add darker colors to a lighter base and not vice versa. In many stencilling projects the base color is white, to which any amount of another japan color can be added or to which smaller quantities of artists' oils can be added for a burst of color. (If you are mixing acrylics, the same rule applies, but you would mix one shade of acrylic paint with another; artists' oils are not suitable colorants for acrylic paint.) Bear in mind the effects of drying and varnishing (discussed on page 30) when trying to match an existing color. It is a good idea to use an index card to record the mixed color and the approximate quantities and shades of paints used so that you can remix and match if you run out.

Colors divide into "warm" and "cool" shades, and the warmth or coolness of a color can be emphasized by mixing. For example, to warm a red you would add yellow; to cool a green you would add blue. French yellow ochre japan color and Naples yellow oil paint are good warming agents. CP green dark and CP green medium japan color will produce cool effects, while CP green light and emerald green will produce warm effects. White, black, and blue will also cool colors.

To subdue a color, you can use lamp black, but raw umber or burnt umber will soften the color more gently, whereas black tends to darken the color. You can also subdue a color by mixing in its complementary color. For example, green will subdue red, orange will subdue blue, violet will subdue yellow, and vice versa.

BACKGROUND COLORS

To test the impact of your choice of colors for your stencils, you must apply them over the exact color of your background, which sometimes will transform the relationship of one color to another within the stencil pattern. Sometimes a color that stands out on white will be absorbed by the background if the colors in the stencil are similar to the background. In other instances a color may be made brighter by its interaction with the background.

This is not to say that you should avoid stencilling against a colored background, but just that you must consider how the background color will affect the colors in your stencil design. Stencilling on a light, preferably white, background will produce the truest colors, but your stencilled outlines will always be conspicuous, bouncing out from the wall. A medium background will absorb some of the color (even after correcting), and from a distance the outlines will appear more muted, creating a veil-like effect

This bathroom stencilled by Mary MacCarthy is an outstanding example of how patterns can be adapted to the space and proportions of a room. *Courtesy* The World of Interiors *(U.K.). Photo by James Mortimer.*

Opposite page: In the eighteenth century, colonists decorated their walls with stencilling, in imitation of lavish European wallpapers such as this one, which was printed from wood blocks. *Courtesy the Victoria and Albert Museum, London.*

CHAPTER THREE
Decorating with Stencils

Flexibility is perhaps the greatest advantage that stencilling has over commercially produced wallpaper and fabrics. Wallpaper comes by the roll and covers the entire wall uniformly, no matter what the idiosyncrasies of the architecture or the proportions of the room. It does not allow for a progression of pattern up a wall or for a stripe of pattern at picture-rail height. Nor can you achieve a denser distribution of pattern to set off a molding, a sloping ceiling, or a door frame. Patterned paper borders are an attempt to overcome this shortcoming of wallpaper patterns, but they do not necessarily complement other elements of pattern within a room. They can look odd placed high on a plain painted wall, especially if the background color of the border does not exactly match the color of the wall. Moreover, border patterns do not always fit in a given space without considerable wastage to achieve a balanced distribution.

Printed wallpapers and fabrics offer you a fixed distribution of pattern, but sometimes a room needs a more diluted pattern scattered over a greater number of surfaces and small areas of dense pattern for particular features. Stencilling offers this flexibility. For example, when decorating a bathroom, you could use a collection of stencilled motifs on a wall to frame a mirror or a window. You could then pick up the same pattern, but in a different configuration, to decorate the sides of the bath or a window shade, dispersing the pattern so that there is more space between the intervening elements. Control over the density and distribution of pattern is a dimension of decorating that ready-made products cannot offer.

Stencilling also offers us the opportunity to experiment with colors before they become permanent. Most of us are obsessed with choosing colors and matching colors when decorating our rooms. The task is often difficult and time-consuming, and we know we will have to live surrounded by our choices. Existing colors, new colors, favorite colors, fabric and wallpaper colors, carpet colors—all pose problems in matching and coordinating. It is perhaps the challenge of color more than any other decorating decision that leads us to seek the help of a professional designer.

When stencilling, however, you can mix any color and try out proofs and samples in their final setting. You can duplicate colors, you can pick out and enhance colors, you can coordinate colors, and you can experiment with contrasting colors. The problems posed by color coordinating can be solved easily when you are applying color with a stencil. A strong color in a carpet and an equally strong but different color in a curtain can be pulled together with a stencil design on the walls that incorporates both. For example, you might have apricot curtains and a medium-blue carpet; a stencil design incorporating both these colors and perhaps a dark red and a deep green for depth and a paler yellow ochre for contrast would link the two separate areas of color within the room.

Stencilling as an Economy

Suppose that you have found a fabric that is prohibitively expensive but irresistible; perhaps it is perfect for a particular setting. In this case, the low cost of stencilling offers an attractive compromise. You can buy the fabric and use it perhaps just for your curtains, and use plain inexpensive fabric for other furnishings within the room. Then, to bring out and strengthen the pattern of the special fabric, you can extract and adapt certain outlines from which you can cut stencils to use in other areas of the room.

If you keep this role of stencilling in mind, you will find yourself less restricted in choosing decorating schemes for your home. Few of us can afford to give free rein to our whims, and for most of us the cost of something is an important factor in our final decision. Decorating just one room in a house is a substantial expense, and decorating every room at once can be financially disastrous. And yet if a house is to become a home, we all have an irresistible urge to leave our imprint in every corner.

MOVING TO A NEW HOUSE

This is particularly true when moving into a new house and inheriting the previous owner's decor. No matter how tasteful, rarely can we wholeheartedly accept it unchanged. If you are lucky, you may have inherited unobtrusive woodwork and walls painted with plain colors. For little money, you can apply stencils to the existing walls and achieve an immediate transformation. A bonus is that stencilling will not cause a great disturbance within your rooms. When you move into a new house, you want to make it home immediately and arrange your furniture in its appropriate setting. Stencilling creates little mess and can be done around the furniture.

If you are not so lucky, and your new house has been decorated previously with patterned wallpapers that clash with your furnishings, stencilling can still offer an economical and immediate solution. You can quickly and inexpensively obliterate the wallpaper with a layer of plain paint, either white or a color, and stencil onto the plain walls.

REDECORATING

Even if you have not moved into a new house, you may be feeling tired of your existing wall decor. The same criteria as when moving can apply, and Carolyn Warrender's project on pages 49–53 demonstrates such an overhaul in detail.

Stencilling as Unique Decoration

Today more and more professional interior designers are looking to stencilling as a means of providing a client with rooms that are custom designed and original. The majority of the artists contributing to this book work with interior designers to provide this kind of decor. Motifs from antique furnishings in a room can be matched with stencilled renderings, while more elaborate stencil treatments can become the focus of a room.

Whether you choose to do your own stencilling or prefer to engage a professional artist is a matter of choice. You may not have the time or energy to carry out the work. Or you may feel that you lack the expertise or adeptness to undertake stencilling your own walls and prefer to rely on the work of skilled craftsmen. In this instance, you will discover a wealth of design ideas from the projects in this book.

Commercial Stencil Patterns

Decorating with stencils has become so popular that manufacturers of printed fabrics and wallpapers are copying traditional stencil motifs. Several companies have based entire collections on stencil patterns, most of which use traditional colorways, or simple configurations of color. These offer the person who does not wish to stencil the opportunity of using stencilling as part of a decorating scheme and an alternative to standard chintz and floral patterns.

Commercially printed fabrics and wallpapers based on stencil patterns also open up further opportunities for you to stencil in your home. You can pick out a stencil motif from a pattern and make your own stencil in any size. Applied to different areas within the same room, it will accent the printed version. Also, a few fabric and wallpaper companies are now specializing in designing collections that tie in with stencils that you can apply yourself. You will find that the range of precut stencils available on the market today is so extensive you will almost always be able to find a design that ties in with an existing fabric or wallpaper pattern. In the project that follows, Carolyn Warrender has done this with a popular pineapple stencil. If you cannot find a precut stencil that is virtually identical to your pattern, choose a close match and adapt it with small details taken from your fabric or wallpaper.

This pineapple motif, which Carolyn Warrender used in the following project, is one example of a precut stencil chosen to coordinate with existing decor.

In the following project, Carolyn Warrender used precut stencils from Stencil-Ease,® ref. no. CL11 (dining room) and ref. no. CL12 (kitchen); and from the Adele Bishop® 1811 House Collection, ref. no. 847 (bathroom and bedroom).

In the dining room, Carolyn Warrender picked up the principal motif from the festoon blind and tablecloth and stencilled a border below the window and at ceiling height. *Photo © Elizabeth Whiting & Associates.*

Carolyn Warrender

Carolyn Warrender founded her thriving London-based interior design business on her fascination with stencilling as a means of decorating. By training she is a designer, with an obvious artistic and creative talent. She became fascinated with stencilling after seeing early examples of the art in the United States. Carolyn chose to learn stencilling as a new skill, but then decided to start a business whereby she could make it accessible to the public at large.

By popularizing stencilling as a decorative medium, Carolyn has often inadvertently introduced her ever-increasing clientele to stencilling as a personally rewarding craft. She wants her clients to see stencilling as a simple solution to decorating and encourages them to take part in the process. She firmly believes that stencilling is one of the quickest, most inexpensive, and most enjoyable ways of transforming a home.

In the following project, Carolyn's purpose is to demonstrate through a sequence of "before" and "after" pictures the various ways in which stencilling can be used to introduce, repeat, and reinforce decorating themes in a home. The location she chose was her own apartment, where she had lived comfortably with her original decor and furnishings for a number of years. An objective look at her surroundings made her realize that, though comfortable, they had become dull and she felt indifferent toward them. Even all-time favorites such as her drawing room wallpaper had lost their immediate impact. It was time for a face-lift.

Starting a new business had meant that both Carolyn's free time and her budget had been severely diverted from her home. She gave herself a week to improve and enliven her entire apartment and came up with the following scheme. Through it we hope that you will be able to see how you can use stencilling as a means of accenting existing furnishings and bringing a new lease on life to old favorites in your home—as well as bringing great satisfaction to yourself.

This project takes a slightly different form from those in subsequent chapters, since it demonstrates decorating ideas rather than a step-by-step project. Lists of materials and instructions are not included. With the exception of the stencil

The dining room before the stencilling was applied. *Photo © Elizabeth Whiting & Associates.*

Detail of the pineapple stencil used under the dining room window. *Photo © Elizabeth Whiting & Associates.*

The hallway of Carolyn's apartment, where a stencilled border was applied near the ceiling to echo the drawing room wallpaper. *Photo © Elizabeth Whiting & Associates.*

Carolyn designed to pick up the pattern of her drawing room walls, all the stencils and materials are commercially available. The details about the stencils are given at the end of the project and can be ordered by mail from the manufacturers or from Stencil Designs Ltd., Carolyn's business (see page 189 for address). The remainder of her equipment and the techniques she has used are the same as those described in Chapter 1.

The project consisted of revamping four rooms and a hallway in Carolyn's apartment—the dining room, the kitchen, the bedroom, the bathroom, and the main hallway. In all except the bedroom Carolyn worked with the existing wall colors and introduced pattern through stencils.

THE HALLWAY

It is easy to overlook a hallway or entranceway and forget that this is the first room in the house that visitors encounter. As a link between rooms, it also bears heavy traffic and therefore can become more of a neglected thoroughfare than an integral part of a home.

A fresh look at the hallway made Carolyn realize that she could make it contribute substantially to the spaciousness of the flat. The existing stippled yellow walls, however, were a marked contrast to the rooms that led off the hall. Carolyn decided to pick up the theme of her drawing room wallpaper, which is heavily patterned, and create a border stencil that she could apply around the walls of the hallway. To make the stencil, she adapted certain details in the wallpaper and duplicated the colors, then applied them to the yellow walls.

In doing this Carolyn achieved two effects. First, the element of pattern in the hallway softens the impact of the drawing room, making the contrast between the two areas less marked. Second, it extends the space of the living room into the hall, making the two areas seem bigger and more connected. There are six doorways leading off the hallway and two pine chests against the walls, and the border pattern helps to pull all of them together.

THE DINING ROOM

In the dining room at the back of the house, the walls were covered with pale green rag-rolled wallpaper, which effectively lightened this otherwise dark room. Carolyn decided to leave the walls intact because painting over them would have destroyed the subtle effect of the rag rolling and applying new wallpaper would have been expensive. The fabric for the festoon blind and tablecloth was also an old favorite, which Carolyn was loath to replace. Its pattern was a small repeating pineapple, reminiscent of the pineapples of early American stencilling.

Carolyn discovered in her shop a precut pineapple motif that closely matched the one in the fabric. She used it to stencil a border below the window, at ceiling height, around and within an archway joining the dining room to the kitchen, and on the panels of the door. She matched the colors of the stencil as closely as she could with the colors of the fabric, using a sage green for the leaves and pale burgundy for the pineapple. The tiny pineapples in the print and the larger pineapples on the walls now work together to carry out the theme of the room, as well as give greater focus to the window and the doorway.

THE KITCHEN

The tiny kitchen leading off from the dining room has stained oak cupboards neatly fitted around all three walls. Even the refrigerator is concealed behind an oak-fronted unit, and there are wooden counters all around. The effect of the wood was rich but almost overpowering in so small a space. Carolyn decided to break up the oak surfaces by applying delicate stencils around the doors and along the edges of the countertops. She used a precut repeating motif and chose sage green and brick colors to echo the colors of the dining room. She left the stained oak surfaces untreated after applying the stencils because she did not want to sacrifice the quality of the wood.

THE BATHROOM

In the bathroom pine paneling had been applied to the sides of the bathtub and other areas. Pine and cane accessories decorated the remainder of the room. So as not to detract from the natural beauty of the wood and the cane, Carolyn chose a small precut leaf-like stencil and applied it using burnt umber thinned to transparency to give the stencilling the effect of a delicately stained inlaid pattern. Stencilling does not have to be executed in opaque colors and can be less obtrusive if the paint is applied thinly and does not detract from the surface underneath—the wood grain in this instance. The stencil was applied randomly over the paneled pine surfaces, and a delicate border added around the top of the bathtub and down the sides of the washbasin fitting.

THE BEDROOM

In the bedroom Carolyn decided to cover the existing green wallpaper with warm peach paint rag-rolled over an off-white ground. She chose the new peach color carefully so that she could retain the printed fabric festoon blind, which she wanted

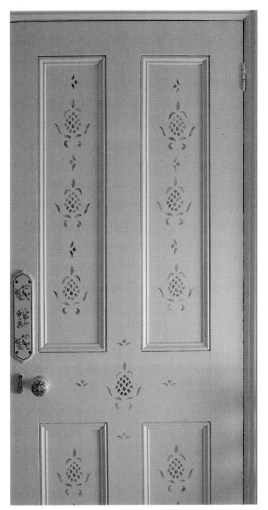

The same pineapple stencil decorates the panels of the dining room door. *Photo © Elizabeth Whiting & Associates.*

Above: **The bathroom before . . .**

Right: **. . . and after. A small stencilled leaf design was applied to the paneled surfaces around the bathtub and washbasin, and another motif was chosen for the wall around the mirror.** *Photos © Elizabeth Whiting & Associates.*

to use as a basis for the new colors in the rest of the room. The bedroom is small and is made even smaller by a wall of fitted closets to one side of the bed. Because the closets are indispensable, Carolyn decided to make them a feature of the room rather than a drawback. She painted the closet doors peach to make them blend with the walls. Then she outlined each door with a floral border stencil that echoed the pattern of her blind and dressing table fabric.

The stencil was a precut Adele Bishop® design that she stocked in her shop, and she executed it in shades of pale green and deep peachy rose. This is an example of how a precut stencil that is similar if not identical can be coordinated with a fabric through its colors. Because the stencil design was applied in specific areas, namely around the cupboard doors and as a border at ceiling height, the two different patterns do not clash, but instead enhance each other.

Perhaps the most notable quality of Carolyn Warrender's project is that, although the apartment is small and condensed, the stencilling is never overpowering. Carolyn's use of borders on walls to add height and airiness to rooms, and of allover patterns in contained areas such as the bathroom, illustrates

Carolyn transformed the bedroom by applying stencils within the doors of the closets. *Photo © Elizabeth Whiting & Associates.*

how stencilling can be used to open up some areas and focus on others. Allover stencilling patterns on the walls of such small rooms would have closed them in even further, while a very tiny border pattern would have seemed fussy in the bathroom. Moreover, one of the greatest successes of the project is the way in which Carolyn managed to retain existing patterns in her home—the drawing room wallpaper, the dining room fabric, and the bedroom fabric, all quite powerful in their settings—and yet introduce additional patterns in the form of stencils without any one of them detracting from another or looking out of place.

Obviously you will be working with different patterns, different geography, and different proportions, but we hope that from Carolyn's example you can get an idea of how stencilling can be used to enhance the existing decor of your home, simply and without any great financial outlay.

a limited area. These include not only specific methods for translating a stencilled pattern onto a small object, but many helpful hints about pattern in general, which can later be applied to larger projects. The method below, which is favored by Tom Burgio, involves working out the distribution of a motif within a specific area and then making an exact reference stencil to fit the surface.

Making and Using a Stencil Key

1. Using your small object (perhaps a canister or a box) as a template, trace the various areas to be stencilled onto tracing paper so that you have a flat record of the areas you will be working within, such as the circular area of a lid, the rectangular shape of the side of a round box, the narrow rectangle of the side of a round lid (see fig. 14). By mapping out the areas, you get an overall two-dimensional idea of the way in which the pattern can be fitted within each surface.

2. Lay one of the traced areas over graph paper, lining it up with the grid on the paper. This will automatically provide you with a scaled reference for the area to be stencilled.

3. With the paper in place over the grid, you can either center an element of the design or repeat a motif equally within the given area. Using the grid lines as a guide, sketch the motif

in pencil on the tracing paper, repeating it as many times as you think will fit. When you have completed the sketch for the entire area, examine it and decide whether you have achieved the right balance of space and motif. You may need to adjust the size of the motif to fit within the space, and again the grid can help. For example, suppose the motif, a heart, is ¼ inch high in the given example, but the border area you are working with is 1 inch deep. To achieve a better proportion, you may need to enlarge the heart to ½ inch high, thus allowing ¼ inch above and below the heart in the finished border. When you have completed your sketch and determined the best size for your motif and the best spacing within the given area, you are ready to make the stencil key.

4. Enlarge or reduce the stencil outline if necessary by means of a photostat or graph paper, as explained in Chapter 1.

5. Using the new enlarged or reduced stencil outline, cut a single stencil from it in acetate or waxed stencil paper. You will be using this as a template, not as a final stencil.

6. Return to your tracing of the area to be stencilled. With the stencil template and a felt-tip pen, draw accurate outlines over the previously sketched outlines on the tracing paper to establish the final size and distribution of the stencils for the area. The outlines should be clear

Figure 14 Traced areas of a canister, in which stencil patterns can be fitted

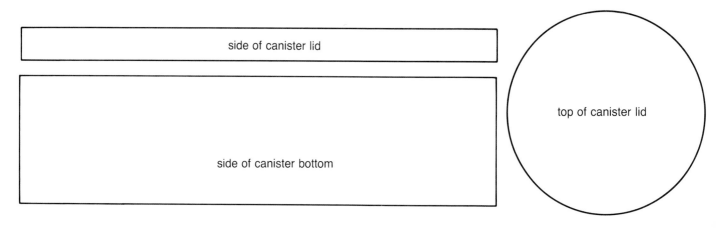

and neat, as this becomes the stencil key from which you will cut an accurate sequence of stencils. Once the stencil key is drawn, make a photocopy of it as a safety measure in case of loss or damage.

7. Lift the traced pattern away from the graph paper and coat the back with rubber cement or spray adhesive. Then stick it onto a piece of smooth illustration board, making sure that the entire surface of the tracing paper adheres to the board. The illustration board will act as a cutting mat. It should be at least 4 inches larger in area than the design you are working with so you can maneuver while cutting the stencils.

8. Cut a piece of waxed stencil paper large enough to allow a 1- to 2-inch border around the stencil pattern. Lay it over the stencil key and hold it in place with masking tape. Using an X-acto® or similar knife, cut the stencil. If the area to be stencilled is small, you can cut stencils for the entire area. If it is larger, you can cut just a section, including registration outlines at either end; because the stencil size and spacing are already established, the stencils will fit the area exactly.

9. Gently lift the stencil paper from the illustration board. As the masking tape peels off, you will find that you have a sequence of accurately cut and positioned stencils that exactly fit within the area to be stencilled. These can then be applied to the surface without further measuring.

DESIGN POSSIBILITIES

This method of working out the pattern for fitting stencils can be used for a variety of purposes. It can be used to fit a simple repeating motif into a border so that it repeats evenly and is the correct size for the border area. It can also be used to fit a design within a circle, perhaps on the top of a lid or on a tray or a circular placemat. Here you would use a circle grid over which you can place the traced area. The grid marks out the various segments of the circle and allows you to work out an even spacing of the design. Such grids are found in special books that contain a library of geometric outlines, published specifically for photocopying. A traced area can also be used to achieve a balanced design when you want it to appear intentionally haphazard.

Christmas tree ornaments, painted Shaker boxes, greetings cards, and wrapping paper have all been stencilled with designs derived from traditional quilt patterns. *Photo by David Arky.*

projects by
Tom Burgio

The stencil patterns for the Christmas tree decorations and boxes in this project are based on traditional American quilt patterns, which Tom Burgio has adapted for a variety of surfaces. Shown here, they conform to a Christmas theme, but the patterns are sufficiently versatile to lend themselves to any occasion or setting if you vary the colors and surfaces.

Tom chose three motifs as the basis for his designs: an eight-pointed star, a patchwork basket, and a laurel-and-hearts medallion. By playing with different sizes and different colors and incorporating them with other simple stencilled forms, he has produced a range of Christmas accessories that are highly original and versatile.

The stencilled boxes are strong, untreated, hardwood boxes, sometimes known as Shaker boxes because of their design. They can be bought in some craft stores or by mail order (see page 189 for suppliers). Because the boxes will probably become keepsakes, you should buy good-quality ones that will warrant the time and care you spend on them. They come in a wide range of shapes and sizes (usually expressed as diameter by height). The three used in the Christmas project are a tallish drum box, a large flat cheese box, and a small flat cheese box. The term *cheese box* derives from the days when cheeses were transported and stored in wooden boxes, as Brie and Camembert still are today. In the second project in this chapter, an oval wooden cheese box is used. All these boxes make useful storage containers; the small flat one can be used on a dressing table for jewelry and other small items, while the large flat box makes a wonderful sewing box. The boxes are not really airtight, and if they are to be used for food, the food should first be sealed in a plastic bag to keep it fresh.

The Christmas tree decorations are an extremely simple and inexpensive way of trimming a Christmas tree. The squares are cut from heavy illustration board and then primed with paint. You will need to buy a whole sheet and cut it up yourself, unless you find a store that sells off-cuts.

In all these projects, with the exception of the glass jars in the final project, acrylic paint is used for the stencilling. Like japan color, acrylic paint is fast-drying, but because it leaves a film or skin as it dries, it is ideal on wooden boxes and cardboard surfaces, making them more durable. Always apply the paint sparingly, with the stencil brush almost dry. A single application will produce a soft, transparent print, while two or more applications will make the coverage opaque. Surfaces (except paper and cardboard) painted with acrylics should be varnished after the paint has dried. A spray varnish is used in these projects because small objects tend to be difficult to hold.

POLKA-DOT DRUM BOX

Whereas stencilling on cards and paper is easy, the boxes require moderate expertise. If you are a beginner, simplify the patterns and colors until you feel comfortable. When you first start stencilling small objects, be as precise as you can without becoming overwhelmed. With practice you will discover your own methods that will make your work much easier.

DEGREE OF DIFFICULTY Moderate

TIME REQUIRED 4 hours: preparing box, ½ hour; making stencils, 1 hour; applying background colors and stencils, 2 hours plus drying times; finishing off, ½ hour

MATERIALS
basic equipment, page 12
drum-shaped wooden box, 7¼″ × 5″
waxed stencil paper
illustration board
leather punch
4 stencil brushes (⅜″–⅝″)
3 flat artists' paintbrushes (¾″–1″)
sandpaper
fine paintbrushes
½ pt. white shellac primer
matte or semi-gloss acrylic spray varnish

ACRYLIC PAINTS
terracotta   dark green
off-white   light green

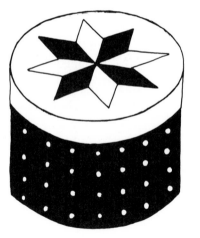

1. Priming the Box
Sand the surface of the box, both outside and inside, using medium-grade sandpaper. Then apply a coat of white oil-based primer (shellac was used here) to both the inside and the outside. Sand again lightly when dry.

The wooden Shaker boxes were painted first to provide an opaque background for the various stencilled patterns. The drum-shaped box was stencilled in a polka-dot and star pattern, while the large and small cheese boxes were done in the same laurel-and-hearts pattern. *Photo by David Arky.*

2. Applying the Background Colors

Base of the box Apply a base coat of terracotta acrylic paint to the outside surface of the box base. When dry, apply a second coat (and possibly a third) so that the surface is well covered and has a shell-like appearance.

Lid of the box Apply two coats of off-white paint to the top of the lid. Then paint the sides of the lid dark green, again using at least two coats of paint. The rim of the white top has a fine dark-green border running around it, which adds a professional touch but is not essential. The border is made in the following way: Around the edge of the top, where the side piece joins it, there is a slight ridge that you can use as a guide for making an even and fine border. Apply masking tape to the top of the lid in small sections, as shown in fig. 15, making sure that all the pieces of masking tape overlap. Then take a utility knife and, following the ridge, cut away the masking tape to reveal the ridge, leaving the white interior masked. Using a fine paintbrush, apply a line of off-white paint to the exposed rim. (If you apply the green right away, it will seep under the masking tape and bleed onto the white. The extra coat of white paint serves to block any seeping paint.) Once the white paint is dry, you can apply the green paint over it, thus forming a fine line around the top of the lid. When it is dry to the touch, lift the masking tape promptly and continue. For a professional finish you can paint the insides also.

Figure 15 Preparing the lid for painting the rim

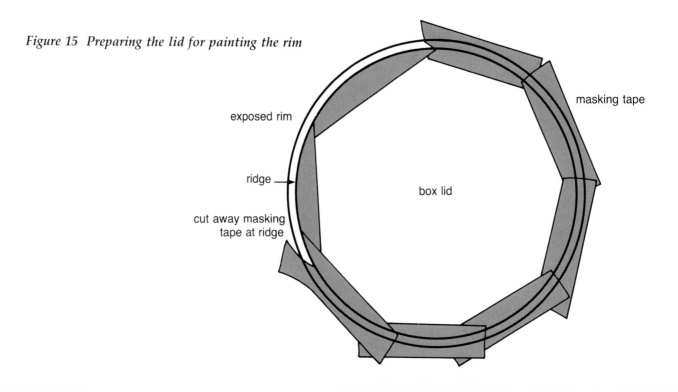

3. Applying the Stencils

The polka-dot stencil for the base is slightly different from a normal stencil because it has been cut with a leather punch and therefore does not require any elaborate knife work. If your box is the same size as the one illustrated, follow the grid supplied. You do not have to cut dots to go all the way around. Instead, you can cut and stencil a portion and then move and register the stencil on the dots you have already painted. If you need to place the dots differently to fit a different-sized box, you can plan out a suitable pattern on graph paper using the squares as a guide and then punch the holes accordingly in your stencil paper. Cut two separate stencils for the lid star.

Base of the box Align the dot stencil around the base, holding it in position with masking tape. Stencil in the dots using off-white paint and apply a second coat, if necessary, before lifting the stencil. To repeat the grid as you go around, use the previously stencilled dots as a register and continue until the entire surface of the base is covered.

Lid of the box Position one of the star stencils over the center of the lid. Hold it in place with masking tape and apply the light green sections, using two coats of paint if necessary. Lift the stencil and position the other star stencil, using the light green outlines as your register. Apply the terracotta paint through this stencil, thus forming the two-colored eight-pointed star.

4. Finishing Off

When the paint is completely dry, apply two coats of acrylic spray varnish to the surfaces. Seal the inside in the same way.

LARGE QUILT-MOTIF BOX
Degree of Difficulty Moderate

Time Required 4 hours, as for previous box

Materials Same as for polka-dot drum box. If you are stencilling both boxes, you will probably have sufficient paint left from the previous project. You will also need:
flat wooden cheese box, 13" × 2¼"
pink acrylic paint

1. Preparing the Box
Prime and sand the box as you did in the previous project.

2. Applying the Background Colors

Base of the box Apply two or three coats of off-white paint to the base and allow it to dry. To create the light green line around the bottom edge, position masking tape ⅜ inch above the bottom edge all around the box. Apply a coat of off-white paint to this masked-off area first to prevent the light green paint seeping under the tape. After this has dried, you can apply one or two coats of light green paint. Remove the masking tape as soon as the paint is dry to the touch.

Lid of the box Apply two coats of off-white paint to the top of the lid. Then paint the sides of the lid pink. To create the pink square border on the top of the lid, find and mark the center of the lid. Draw a faint pencil or chalk line across the center to mark the diameter of the lid (see fig. 16). Draw another line at right angles to this one. Using the four points so formed on the edge of the lid, place masking tape between the points to form a square that touches the edge of the lid. Then apply a piece of masking tape ¾ inch in from one side of the masking tape square. Apply pink paint between these two pieces of tape to form the first side of the pink border, then remove the tape. Apply a piece of masking tape to the next side of the square, again ¾ inch in. Apply pink paint to make the second side and repeat until the border is complete. When the paint is dry, place masking tape over this pink border and paint in the light green areas on the outside, taking care that no white shows through where the pink and green areas meet.

Figure 16 Applying the stripe border to the lid

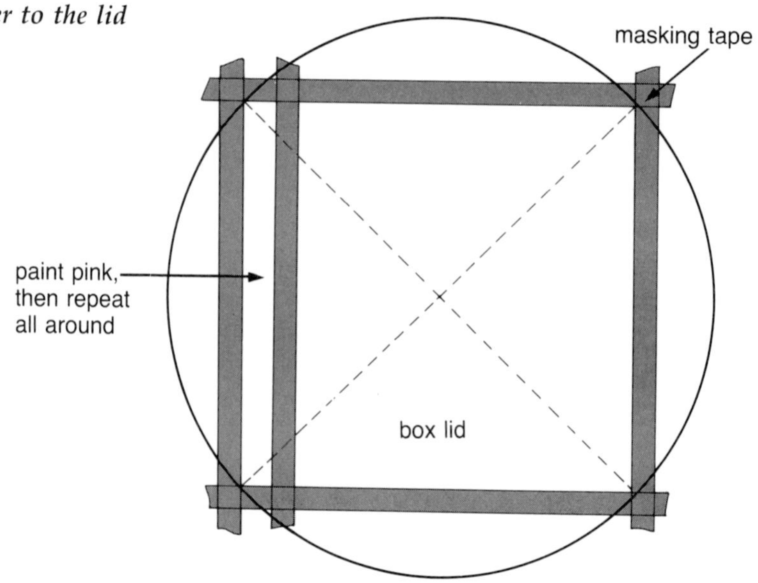

masking tape

paint pink,
then repeat
all around

box lid

3. Cutting the Stencils

If your box is the same size as the one illustrated, you can trace the stencils directly from the outlines given. If you are using a different-sized box, scale the patterns up or down accordingly and make stencil keys as described on page 56. You should have three stencils in all: the laurel-and-hearts for the top of the lid, the scallop-and-pendant border for the sides of the lid, and hearts for the sides of the base. Cut pieces of waxed stencil paper 2 inches larger all around than each stencil outline and cut out the stencils.

4. Applying the Stencils

Base of the box Using the repeating heart stencil for the base, stencil the hearts with terracotta paint, positioning them so that their points are ¼ inch above the light green border. When you have completed the first sequence of hearts, use the last stenciled heart as a register and repeat the hearts around the outside of the box base.

Lid of the box After masking out the areas for the pendants with masking tape, apply the scallop stencil in light green around the lid's sides, again using the scallops you have already stenciled as a register. When the paint is dry, remove the masking tape from the pendant areas and, using dark green paint, stencil in the pendants all around the lid sides.

Position the laurel-and-hearts stencil over the center of the lid, masking out the four heart outlines. Stencil in the leaf design with dark green paint. Leave the stencil taped in position and lift the masking tape from over the hearts. Stencil in the hearts with terracotta paint.

5. Finishing Off

Follow the instructions for the polka-dot drum box.

SMALL QUILT-MOTIF BOX

The small quilt-pattern box is made in exactly the same way as the large one, except that the stencils are scaled down to the proportions of the box and cut accordingly. It will take approximately 3 to 4 hours to complete. You will need a small wooden cheese box, 6¼ inches by 2 inches.

CHRISTMAS TREE MEDALLIONS

DEGREE OF DIFFICULTY Easy

TIME REQUIRED 3 hours: cutting and preparing medallions, 1 hour; making stencils, ½ hour; applying background colors and stencils, 1 hour; finishing off, ½ hour

MATERIALS Same as for quilt-motif boxes, plus:
1 sheet smooth-surface illustration board
leather punch
matte or semi-gloss acrylic spray varnish
ribbon for hanging

1. Cutting and Priming

Cut the illustration board into twelve squares 3½ inches
by 3½ inches. Sand the cut edges and then prime each square
with white shellac on both sides. Allow to dry.

2. Applying the Background Color

Paint four of the squares off-white on both sides, four pink
on both sides, and the remaining four terracotta. The off-white
squares have a terracotta border, the pink squares an off-white
border, and the terracotta squares a pink border. To apply these
borders, mark points ¼ inch in from each corner of the squares.
Apply a strip of masking tape between two of these points on
one side, positioning the tape to the inside of the points (see
fig. 17). Paint the border with the appropriate color and remove
the masking tape. Follow the same procedure for the remaining
sides until the border is complete.

Figure 17 Painting the borders of the medallions

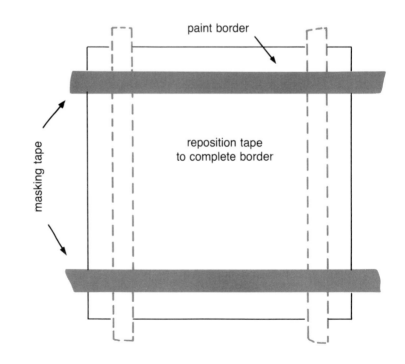

3. Cutting the Stencils

Trace the three stencil outlines and cut pieces of stencil paper for each, allowing a 2-inch border all around. Cut out the stencils.

4. Stencilling the Motifs

Mark the center of each square on the side with the border. Position the appropriate stencil so that it aligns with the center and secure it with masking tape. Stencil the pattern in place, using two coats of paint if necessary. The basket goes on the terracotta center, the eight-pointed star on the pink center, and the laurel-and-hearts medallion on the off-white center. (You can, if you wish, repeat the stencilling process on the back of the medallions.)

5. Finishing Off

Coat each square with varnish on both sides. Stamp a hole in one corner of each square with the leather punch. Tie a loop through this hole with the ribbon.

WRAPPING PAPER

Wrapping paper is stencilled in a much more haphazard way. In this case the parcel was wrapped in plain paper and the stencil design applied to fit the shape of the parcel. Acrylic paint was used on a gloss-coated paper. The design was roughly mapped out so that it balanced, but arduous measuring was unnecessary. This design lends itself to a symmetrical layout, but on many stencil projects you can work out the pattern and repeat as you go along. You can use almost any paper, from brown wrapping paper to the most expensive parchment. Use any of the designs given here for the stencilled medallions or devise your own stencil patterns. You can use acrylic or tempera paint, marker pen, even wax or lead crayon. Similarly, you can stencil the paper before wrapping the present.

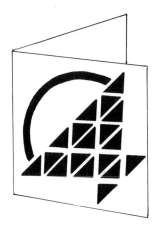

GREETING CARDS AND STATIONERY

Greeting cards offer a similarly wide range of design possibilities. In the case of this project, the basket and eight-pointed star patterns were stencilled with felt-tip marker onto white card, but you could use acrylic paint instead. Almost any of the patterns given in this book would work well as card designs and you'll find many more in your own sources. Use a firm card and cut it to size before applying the stencil. Remember that masking tape can tear the surface of the card if applied too firmly, and you should avoid using it if possible. Stencilling also provides an original and economical means of producing your own personalized stationery. Use any type of writing paper and stencil with a relatively dry brush so that the paint does not buckle the paper surface.

A detail of the stencilled rosebud, showing how the paint is shaded and blended in both the flower and the leaves. *Photo by David Arky.*

BLUE ROSEBUD BOX AND PICTURE FRAME

Using a simple oval wooden Shaker box and a commercial wooden picture frame, you can make a unique and beautiful dressing table set, as pictured on page 54. By choosing colors to coordinate with your own decorating scheme, you can transform even the simplest of dressing tables.

The box is painted and stencilled in the same way as the previous wooden boxes, using acrylic paints. Neither the rosebud nor the lattice border stencil patterns require scaling up or down if you are using the same size box as the one illustrated (7½″ × 5¾″ × 3⅜″). For the rosebud you need two different arrangements of the pattern: one for the sides of the base and one for the top of the lid. If your box is a different size, follow the instructions on page 56 for arranging a motif within a certain area.

If your picture frame is not already painted, sand it if necessary and then prime it. When dry, apply two coats of oil-based paint (gloss or semi-gloss). Remove the picture mat from the frame and apply two or more coats of acrylic paint to it. Using the rosebud stencil, apply two rosebuds around the upper left corner and two around the bottom right corner of the mat.

The frame is now complete. Insert a picture and reassemble the frame.

WOODEN CANISTER

Stencilling containers or utensils is a quick and effective way of livening up any kitchen. Here Tom Burgio has used a simple tulip design in a variety of ways and on a variety of surfaces. The possibilities are endless; you can stencil anything from wooden chopping boards to ceramic and glass containers. Utensils that will get a lot of use must be well sealed, and there are special paints available for stencilling onto plates and other dishes that will be frequently used and washed. In general, your projects will be more successful if you reserve stencilling for articles that will be decorative or lightly used and for the outsides of containers, tins, and canisters.

A wooden canister and two glass storage jars have been decorated with coordinating stencil patterns. *Photo by David Arky.*

DEGREE OF DIFFICULTY Easy

TIME REQUIRED 2½ hours: preparing canister, ½ hour; making stencils, 1 hour; applying stencils, ½ hour; finishing off, ½ hour

MATERIALS Same as for previous projects, plus: wooden canister, 6¼″ × 6″

ACRYLIC PAINTS

yellow ochre	green
red	blue

1. Preparation and Background

Sand the surface of the lid and the base. Apply a thin, wash-like coat of yellow ochre paint (three parts water to one part paint) to the outside of the lid and the base.

Stick masking tape all around the side of the lid, ⅜ inch up from the edge, and paint the edge green. Remove the masking tape when the paint is dry. Around the base apply a red border ¼ inch up from the bottom edge.

2. Cutting the Stencils

Following the scale of the stencil outlines given (unless using a canister of a different size), trace one outline of the large tulip and butterfly pattern for the base and one outline of the smaller tulip pattern for the lid. Using the same method as for the previous boxes, cut stencils in waxed stencil paper for the outlines.

3. Applying the Stencils

Base of the canister Turn the canister base upside down and mark the center of the bottom. Then divide the bottom into quarters and mark each quarter on the perimeter of the base. Using these markings as a guide, mark the four quarters on the sides of the canister. Position a large tulip and butterfly stencil over one of these markings, directly above the red border. Mask off the red flower and butterfly and apply the green section of the stencil. Repeat for the other three tulip stencils. Then stencil in the red flowers on each of the four tulips, and finally the blue butterflies.

Lid of the canister Remove the knob from the top of the canister and mark the center of the top of the lid. Mask off the flower areas of the lid stencil. Center the stencil on the lid and paint in the green leaves. Lift the masking tape and paint in the red flowers.

4. Finishing Off

Apply two coats of matte varnish to the outside and the inside of the lid and the base. Attach the knob to the lid.

GLASS STORAGE JARS

Using an enamel paint of the type used for model making, you will be able to stencil directly onto glass and the paint will not wash or wear off. Both jars illustrated here have been stencilled in this way, using a smaller version of the tulip pattern used for the wooden canister. In the case of the larger jar, the stencils were applied haphazardly, whereas on the smaller jar,

they were applied in a straight line. In each case, the stencilling is easy, and the same techniques can readily be applied to other glass surfaces. Mirrors, drinking glasses, pitchers, glass bowls— even windows—all respond well to this treatment. The same paint can also be applied to plastic containers, making a wealth of designs possible for picnic equipment and outdoor plates and containers. Always apply the paint to the outside of the item you are stencilling, and be sure to allow sufficient time for this slower-drying paint to dry before moving from one color to the next.

DEGREE OF DIFFICULTY Easy

TIME REQUIRED 1 hour: making stencils, ½ hour; applying stencils, ½ hour

MATERIALS Same as for previous projects, plus:

1 tube red enamel paint
1 tube green enamel paint
1 small and 1 large glass storage jar

Larger Glass Jar
Clean the surface of the jar thoroughly with detergent. Cut several separate stencils from the outline given and mask off the red flower area of the tulip. Work out roughly the way in which you will arrange the flowers on the surface of the jar. (It is not necessary to mark the surface; simply get an idea of the distribution.)

With green paint, apply the stencils, turning them as you wish and remembering to allow space for the flowers. Hold the stencils lightly in place with masking tape as you paint. When you have completed all the green areas and the paint has dried, stencil in the red flowers. There is no need to seal this paint surface.

Small Glass Jar
A simple line of tulips decorates the small glass jar. To mark the straight line around the jar, use a wax crayon and a piece of pliable acetate, stencil paper, or a tape measure to draw against. After masking out the flower areas, position the stencil on the line and stencil in the green areas, repeating the leaves and the stems around the jar. Finish off with the red flowers. To give an attractive finish to the jar, you can cut a simple round of matching fabric, slightly larger than the lid, and anchor it over the lid with ribbon.

Use same size

Use same size

Use same size for Large Quilt-Motif Box.   Reduce 45% for Small Quilt-Motif Box.

Use same size

Use same size

Use same size

Use same size

Use same size

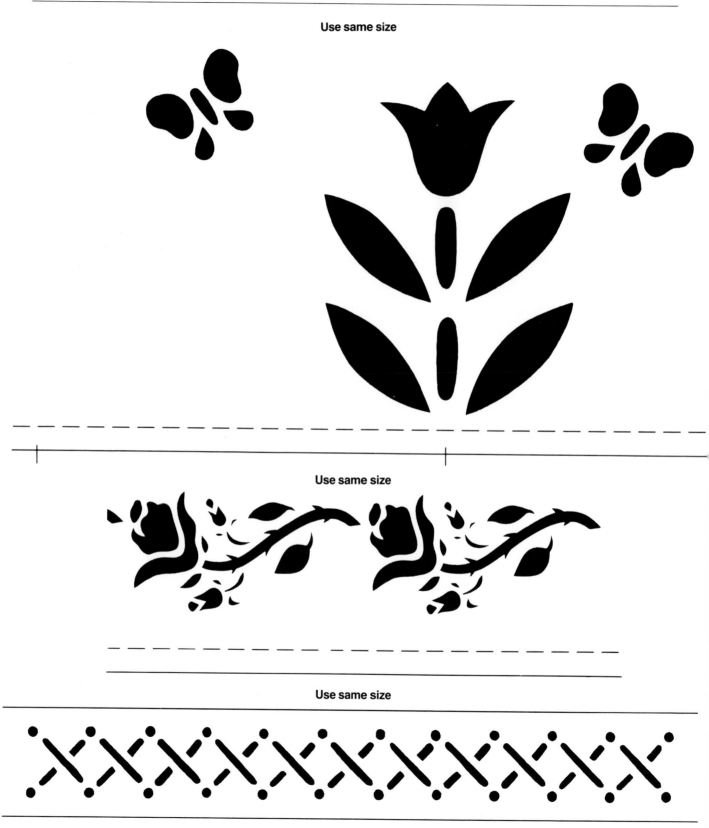

Use same size

Use same size

Use same size

Use same size

The pattern for the stencilled frieze done by Tina Leith for her London house was influenced by the Marianne North room at Kew. *Courtesy* The World of Interiors *(U.K.). Photo by James Wedge.*

Opposite page: This border of birds and flowers, stencilled by Virginia Teichner, was inspired by Indian crewel work and lends itself well to the antique furnishings. Virginia also stencilled the floor using a historic pattern from Adele Bishop Inc. *Photo by David Arky.*

78

CHAPTER FIVE
Borders

Perhaps the most versatile of all stencilled forms, a border can be as simple and unsophisticated or as complex and elaborate as you like. A stencilled border can be applied to all kinds of surfaces to improve proportions, to indicate boundaries, or simply to add ornamentation. Borders have always been an integral part of more involved stencilling projects. Rarely would a wall be stencilled without incorporating some sort of stencilled border to contain the design. Similarly, stencilled floors in the past frequently included a border, and indeed some floors would have a broad stencilled border surrounding a plain, central area. On stencilled furniture a partial or continuous border was frequently added to provide a neat and definitive edge to the various motifs contained in a piece.

In this chapter, however, we are concerned with using the border as a distinct form of decoration, separate from its role within more elaborate projects. Borders can be used to enhance floors, walls, window and door frames, simple floorcloths, tabletops, chair backs, chests of drawers and cupboards, staircases, shelves, sta-

tionery, placemats, headboards, small boxes, trays, curtains and bedcoverings, and picture frames, to name but a few. A border can be executed in a couple of hours, or it can be an involved and detailed project requiring hours of careful artistry.

The appeal of a stencilled border lies in its subtle yet integrated way of bringing decoration into a room or an object, without the overpowering effect of an overall design. A hand-painted border allows you to pick up only a few elements of pattern from a furnishing, such as a curtain or a pillow, and apply them to a particular feature or area in a room. Borders also serve as a means of introducing small touches of contrasting design into a room. For example, by using a geometric border, you can subtly counteract an otherwise floral or plain decorating scheme.

A border can also be used to enhance or disguise existing architectural features. For example, the proportions of a room can be effectively altered by the introduction of a stencilled border. A ceiling that seems too high can be successfully lowered by placing a narrow border at picture-rail height, thereby focusing the eye lower on the wall. The room's proportions can be further altered by stencilling in another identical or modified border at chair-rail height, thereby breaking up the expanse of wall twice. If, however, your room needs heightening because the ceiling is too low, stencilling borders to form vertical panels on the walls will improve the pro-portions. A border stencilled either above a baseboard or in place of a baseboard has the effect of adding weight to the room at floor level. Always remember, however, that too much separation of wall areas by means of decorative borders will confuse and overpower the eye. If you want overall decoration of a surface, you should use the border as a boundary and expand

A fine stencilled border designed by Virginia Teichner accents the chair rail and doorways in this classic hallway. *Photo by David Arky.*

Detail of the border pattern. *Photo by David Arky.*

your pattern into an overall wall pattern.

Sloping ceilings and walls can be enhanced by running a simple border along the wall just below ceiling height. Arches and doorways frequently benefit from the application of a delicate border running around them, from the floor level upward. A window that requires a simple treatment, such as a plain blind to allow maximum light, can be delicately decorated with a simple border running around the outside of the frame and a matching border running across the bottom of the blind.

Staircases are particularly well-suited to border treatment. A stencilled border running down the outside of a stairwell wall, parallel to the banister rail, has an impact similar to that of a stencilled border on a sloping ceiling. Or a border can be applied down the inside wall of the staircase, just above the baseboard. Perhaps most effective of all is the use of stencils on the stair risers. If you cannot afford stair carpeting or prefer to leave your staircase of natural or painted wood, you can create a very pretty and unusual effect by applying a border across the stair risers. Stencilled borders can make a staircase become an important decorative feature in any house,

Pattern Sources

The patterns you use for a border design, like other stencil designs, can come from all manner of sources. In fact, for a border the task is easier. It is much simpler to envision the effect of a border pattern than that of an overall wall design, and it is similarly much simpler to select details from a design source and envision them as a repetitive border pattern than to compose an allover configuration. Ceramics provide a wealth of design possibilites. Look around the edges of old plates and cups for suitable outlines. You will find that old tiles are another good source of patterns.

Architectural pediments and friezes offer wonderful border outlines, as do the carved wooden borders found on furniture, door frames, and pediments. Look at old patchwork quilts for

Lynn Goodpasture stencilled a border at chair-rail height around a room and then adapted the pattern for a lampshade. *Photo by David Arky.*

dogtooth and checkerboard borders, as well as appliquéd outlines such as swags and flowers, which can be translated into effective border patterns. Veneers on furniture often take the form of a border pattern, sometimes being simple and geometric, sometimes imitating trailing vines and flowers. Woven rugs and textiles frequently incorporate simple borders to act as a boundary to the progressive patterns within.

Early Egyptian and Greek art frequently incorporate borders of geometric or key patterns, and examples of these can be found on museum postcards and other reproductions of the pieces. Islamic art uses a variety of border techniques that also work well when broken down into stencil form.

This group of borders by Virginia Teichner shows just a few of the design possibilities available to stencillers. *Photos by David Arky.*

Perhaps the most fun of all is to use borders for decorating children's rooms. Your children's favorite books and toys can provide readily identifiable outlines you can adapt into stencil form. A bathroom or nursery becomes a haven to a child who is surrounded by his or her favorite characters. And the beauty of stencilling a border is that it can be inexpensively updated or replaced as a child grows.

Stencilled borders can also be used in a *trompe l'oeil* manner to introduce architectural ornaments into rooms with plain walls and ceilings. An effective dentil border can be applied using stencilled squares to give a three-dimensional effect around the top of a wall, as in the project in Chapter 9. A simulated plaster relief frieze can be stencilled between a picture rail and the ceiling. Similar relief and three-dimensional effects can be stencilled onto furniture to imitate carving and molding.

Techniques for Applying Borders

Stencilling borders onto a surface requires several techniques that are peculiar to borders alone. These are touched on in Chapter 1 but are explained more fully here.

FITTING THE PATTERN
TO THE SPACE

The first problem most people face is how to fit a border pattern into a given space. There are two basic types of borders: those that run continuously and those that have an obvious repeat. Borders that run continuously and contain one simple, repeating motif have little need for exact measuring and preplanning. Usually you can start stencilling at one end and continue until you reach the other end. Examples would include a simple repeating vine, a geometric border, or a dentil border. When a border is made up of a repeating motif with obvious spacing in between or a more complex repeating design, you must measure the space that the border is to fill and work out exactly how many repeats you can accommodate and how much space you

should leave between repeats. To do this, you must also consider the size of the motif or border pattern you choose. How much you enlarge or reduce a border pattern will be affected by the amount of vertical space you wish the pattern to occupy. If you want a deep border, you will need to enlarge the outline until it reaches the depth you require. Similarly, if you want a very narrow border, you must reduce it accordingly. With this dimension established, you can then start to work on the spacing and repeating of the outline.

Let us consider first the simplest outline, consisting of a single repeating motif such as a rosette. Suppose that your wall is 12 feet long and you want the rosette to be 6 inches in diameter. By experimenting with a proof of the motif on paper, you decide that a minimum of 4 inches should be allowed between each rosette and that, if possible, you would like this 4-inch space to appear at either end of the wall, before the corner is reached. Overall, you have a length of 144 inches to play with. Each unit of the design (one rosette and one space) occupies 10 inches (6″ + 4″). You must first subtract 4 inches from the 144 inches to allow for the extra space

Figure 18 Simple rosette for a border

you require at the end of the run, giving you 140 inches to play with. Dividing 140 inches by 10 inches gives you 14 repeats of the design.

If, however, a rosette of 5 inches diameter would be more suitable, with an intervening space of 3 inches, your calculations will be slightly more complicated. Each element will then occupy 8 inches and you will need an extra 3 inches at the end. So you have 141 inches (144″ − 3″) divided by 8 inches. This comes to approximately 17½ repeats. By adding an extra ¼ inch to each space, you will overcome having extra blank space. The idea behind these calculations is to achieve a balanced design without having to adhere to strict accuracy. Always remember that the beauty of stencilling lies in its handcrafted effect; so long as the eye is satisfied, there is no need for meticulous measuring.

With your basic calculations worked out, you can start to apply your border. As explained on pages 23–25, this can be done either by finding the center of the expanse to be stencilled or by working from one end. The design will be more balanced if you start at the center and work to either side, unless you know from your calculations that the pattern exactly fits.

Whether you decide to center your design in the middle of each expanse of border, taking the consequences of having partial repeats at the corners, or to start at one end and work around, mechanically repeating the pattern wherever the repeat falls, is a matter of taste. It will depend to a great extent on the design. If the design is particularly conspicuous and bold, it will be more pleasing if it is centered. Again, enlarging and reducing the design can help accommodate all dimensions, and you might be able not only to center the design, but also to finish at the corners on a complete repeat.

Whatever your pattern and whatever your surface, when you first begin stencilling, you should sketch and plan the design on paper before setting off. Only with the simplest of borders is it both fun and safe to stencil directly onto the surface without planning out the design beforehand.

MEASURING AND MARKING A BORDER

Once you have decided on the depth of your border design and the amount of space you want on either side of the border, you are ready to mark it out on the surface. If the border is horizontal, you will need a yardstick or ruler, a T-square or right angle, and a chalk or soft-lead pencil. If the border is to go around a wall, measure down from the ceiling or up from the baseboard and mark its position with a pencil dot every 9 inches or so along the surface. If the border is to be on a flat surface such as a floor or on a piece of furniture, again allow for any space outside the border and measure in from the wall or from the edge of the piece. Then join all the dots with a light continuous line, allowing for the cornering technique you choose (see below). You will use the line to register your stencil.

When you join up the individual dots, especially for a wall or a floor border, you may find that the line curves because the walls are not straight. In this case, it is best to straighten the line to compensate for the curvature of the wall. If you allow the pattern to follow the curvature of the wall, the inconsistencies will be emphasized and your stencilling will look inaccurate. Use a spirit level on a wall as a guide.

If you wish to place a border vertically, you will need to use a plumb line and chalk box so that it will fall in a straight vertical line (see page 25). If the border is simply surrounding a door or a window frame, then measure from the edge of the frame in the same way as for a horizontal border.

TURNING CORNERS

Applying a stencilled border frequently entails turning a corner. In the case of a floor, the top of a piece of furniture, a frame, a floorcloth, or an outlined panel, turning a corner means taking the border around a right angle, which requires some form of mitering or breaking of the design. There are three basic ways of taking a pattern around a corner.

Blocking

The simplest way to turn a corner is to stencil almost to the end in one direction, stopping at the inside edge of the border that will go in the other direction. Then turn the stencil at a right angle and start the pattern again at the edge of the previously stencilled border. Mask the end of the first border so that you do not overlap the second strip of border on it. Blocking interrupts the pattern so that it does not flow around the corner, but it is quick and uncomplicated. You would also use this method if you were taking a solid stripe around a corner. (See the stencilled floor in Chapter 10, where a corner motif has also been introduced.)

reaches at an angle into the corner. Wait for the paint to dry and then move the tape or acetate to the other side of the line so that the previously stencilled area is masked. Now start stencilling up in the corner so that the two sides of the pattern meet at an angle.

Continuous Pattern

If your border pattern is quite detailed and fluid, you will be able to adapt it so that the corner appears as an intentional progression of the design. This is particularly feasible when you are stencilling a floral design with curved stems that can be blended easily around a corner. You may need to block out some areas of the design

Figure 20 Mitered corner

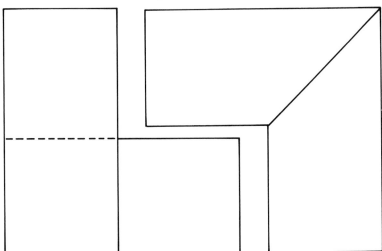

Figure 19 Blocked corner

Figure 21 Taking the pattern around a corner

Mitering

Mitering is the most professional way to turn a corner because it provides a gentle and inconspicuous join. When you sketch out your lines for the position of a border, draw a diagonal line from the point where the two inner lines intersect to the corner where the two outer lines intersect. Place masking tape or a strip of acetate held in position with masking tape along this line opposite the side on which you are stencilling. Stencil up to the tape so that the pattern

and add others, and be sure that any curvature in the design goes out to fill the corner rather than bending inward and cutting it short.

Turning a Corner in a Wall

When you are stencilling a border around a wall, you will often need to continue the pattern around a corner with no evidence of a join. To do this, you must gently bend your stencil at the point in the pattern where the corner falls. Then use a piece of plain acetate to mask the part of the stencil that wraps around onto the next wall, and stencil up to the corner. Lift the acetate and mask the area that has just been stencilled while you continue around the corner.

BORDERING A CURVED EDGE

To print a border around a circular top such as a table or tray, you must be sure your pattern fits the proportions of the area to be stencilled. You can best do this either by using a tiny motif and repeating it at regular intervals around the edge, or by making a stencil key, as described in Chapter 4. To make a stencil key, you need to trace the area or a segment of it onto paper. Then draw the border area to the inside of this tracing and sketch out the pattern to fit the curve of the circle. You can then cut a curved section of stencil corresponding to a segment of the design and apply it repetitively around the edge.

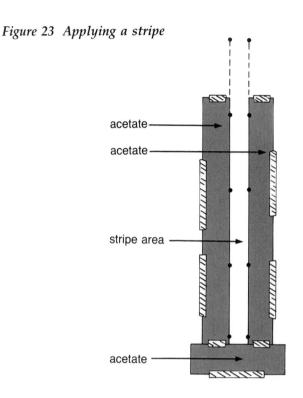

Figure 23 Applying a stripe

APPLYING A STRIPE

A stripe or solid band of color is also a type of border frequently used around a floor (see Chapter 10), on a floorcloth (see Chapter 6), a piece of furniture, or a wall. It can be used in conjunction with a more elaborate border pattern or in place of a border pattern, and it can be as fine or as wide as you choose.

It is important to mark out a stripe before you start to apply paint. Marking out a stripe with a plumb line on a floor is described in full in Chapter 10. On a smaller flat surface or a wall surface, mark out the stripe with pencil or chalk dots and join them to make two parallel lines, just as you would mark out a registration line for any border. Again, it is important that the line is straight and that any idiosyncrasies of the edge or the wall surface are taken into account.

To paint in the stripe, you need two long lengths (24 to 30 inches) of .010-grade acetate. Cut these so that you have a precut edge to stencil against and not your own edge, which will not be as straight. Tape one of the sheets of acetate firmly to the surface so that the precut edge

Figure 22 Making a stencil section for bordering a circular surface

aligns with one of the indicated lines. Then tape the other piece of acetate along the other side of the stripe in the same manner. Block the end of the stripe with a straight-edged scrap of acetate. Stencil in your paint as usual, working your way down the stripe with a circular motion of the brush and replenishing your paint if it dries out. Try to apply the paint evenly. When you reach the end of a run, move both strips of acetate along, aligning them carefully, until the stripe is complete.

To turn a corner in a stripe, stencil up to one edge and then turn at right angles, but mask the end you have already stencilled with a scrap of acetate so that you do not have two coats of paint in the corner.

SETTING UP A WORK SPACE

If you are stencilling a border around a wall, a floor, or a door or window frame, you will need to assemble your stencilling materials on a small portable table. Stencilling a border high up can be very strenuous work. You will need a sturdy stepladder, which you will keep moving around the room as you progress. Do not attempt to do too much at once. Continually reaching upward will tire your arms as well as your eyes. If possible, work in daylight and divide the project into sections that can be completed in stages. Do not attempt to stencil a high border if you do not like working high up.

Taking Care of a Stencilled Border

Once dry, a stencilled border on a wall can be sponged clean with soap and warm water. Abrasives should not be used because they will lift the paint. Once a border has been stencilled in a room, many people are reluctant to lose it, but eventually walls do need repainting. Fortunately, when the border is high up, it rarely comes to any harm—even though the rest of the wall may be scratched and marked. In the case of the animal border in the following project, it is easy to redecorate up to the line of grass, masking the grass as you paint up to it. In the case of the birds-and-flowers border, it would be difficult to paint up to the curving outlines of the vines, flowers, and birds. There are two solutions. You can match the existing paint as best you can (which may not be too difficult if the paint is off-white, as here), taking the new paint up to a horizontal line just below the lowest elements of the design. Or if you want to paint the walls a new color, you can apply a very fine horizontal stripe an inch or so below the border in a dark coordinating color and then paint the new color up to this line.

If your border is at baseboard or chair-rail height, it is more susceptible to chipping and scratching. It is a good idea to keep a record of the colors you used, along with your stencils, so that areas can be touched up or stencilled again if necessary.

Virginia Teichner's design for a simple border of birds, animals, and trees transforms a room into a colorful nursery. The border runs around the room at picture-rail height. *Photo by David Arky.*

projects by
Virginia Teichner

The first of Virginia Teichner's designs is a border for a children's room. The primitive animal forms were inspired by old appliquéd quilt designs and juvenile illustrations. The outlines are simple and can be applied in any sequence, as long as a balanced pace is maintained. The beauty of these outlines is that, although used here in a border, they lend themselves to almost any stencilling treatment. They would work well on fabric to make a stencilled quilt, comforter, or pillow, applied in either a random or a measured pattern, with the grass edge as a border. The outlines are also ideal for stencilling onto furniture—chests of drawers, fitted cupboards, tabletops, chairs, stools, and headboards. The border could be reproduced, exactly as it appears here, on a dust ruffle to coordinate with the border around the ceiling.

These outlines would also be effective in a children's bathroom. They could be stencilled around the sides of a bathtub with panel sides or used in a floor pattern. They could be stencilled on a blind at a window.

The pattern has no obvious repeat. The grass border is applied first and the animals and trees are arranged afterward according to the available space. Last of all come the clouds and birds, which can be scattered within the pattern. If you apply the paint thinly, the wash-like effect will counteract the solid forms of the animals. Blend and shade the paint as you apply it for a deeper effect.

When Virginia executed this design, she did not assign a specific color to a specific motif but instead assembled a palette from which all the stencilled forms were painted. She applied the colors so that they balanced but were not rigidly repetitive. Several of the outlines require two stencils and can therefore be stencilled in two different colors. As a border, the design works best in a high-ceilinged room, running at least 10 inches below the ceiling. It is a good idea to leave space above the animal outlines for the clouds and birds to occupy. If you have a picture rail, you can rest the border on it so that the grass border grows up from the rail.

A detail of the outlines shows how the paint is delicately shaded on the surface. *Photo by David Arky.*

**Taking the border pattern around
a corner of the room.** *Photo by
David Arky*.

4. Applying the Stencils

Mix a saucer of green paint for the grass using medium green japan color as a base and tinting it if you wish. Thin to the correct consistency with turpentine. Secure the grass border stencil firmly to the wall with masking tape, aligning it with the pencil line. Stencil in the first section of grass. Continue around the room, registering the stencil, until the grass is complete.

Mix saucers of red, blue, brown, and yellow paint, tinting and thinning until you achieve the colors and consistency you want. Take the tree trunk stencil and apply it at approximately 24-inch intervals in different colors around the grass border so that the trunks just rest on the grass. Then stencil in the leaves of the tree in contrasting colors.

Apply the animal stencils, using different colors as you work along and first stencilling in the main bodies and then going back to apply the horses' manes and tails, the ducks' feet and beaks, the cats' patches, the giraffes' spots, and the leaves on the trees in contrasting colors. The elephants' toes and eyes can be painted freehand. Shade the paint subtly to prevent solid blocks of color.

With all the animals in place, stencil in the clouds and birds randomly to fill the design, again using a full range of colors. As you stencil in the clouds, use very little paint and shade it to give a cloud-like effect.

The border is now complete and does not require a varnish coat.

BIRDS-AND-FLOWERS BORDER

This is a more complicated border than the animal border because of the lengthy repeat of the design and the more intricate coloration of the birds and flowers. It is still relatively easy to execute and would be appropriate not only in a bedroom, as shown here, but also in a living room, dining room, or hallway. To simplify the design, you could omit the bird outlines and simply have a repeating flower border.

The design was inspired by Indian crewelwork, although similar outlines can be found in printed textile and appliquéd quilts. It works best in a high-ceilinged room against a contrasting background. This is an imposing border, so for a smaller room the design should be reduced. The pattern would also work well on a floorcloth or as a fabric border.

If you include the birds, you will use six colors, which can be varied according to your color scheme. The colors listed here are the basic ones needed to achieve the colors Virginia used. When you stencil in the birds, use the same basic vine stencil, but omit the flowers in the areas where the birds sit and stencil in two birds facing each other instead.

DEGREE OF DIFFICULTY Moderate

TIME REQUIRED 2–3 days: making stencils, ½ day; measuring and marking walls, ½ day; stencilling, 1–2 days, depending on room size

A sample run of the design shows a collection of the animal, bird, and cloud outlines grouped on the grass border and falling between two trees. The border rests just below the picture rail in this room. *Photo by David Arky.*

MATERIALS Same as for previous project.

JAPAN COLORS
flake white
lamp black
CP green dark
chrome yellow medium

Venetian red
Prussian blue
French yellow ochre

1. Preparing the Surface
Paint the entire wall with a flat latex or semi-gloss oil-based paint if necessary. The walls should be smooth, although a very soft effect can be achieved by stencilling the design over a matte sand paint.

2. Preparing the Stencils
Enlarge the stencil outlines as indicated or as you desire; when scaled up, the border measures 10 inches deep. You may wish to adjust this according to the size of your room. Cut pieces of acetate for each stencil, allowing at least 2 inches extra around each outline. Trace the enlarged outlines onto the acetate, using a drawing pen. Include registration outlines wherever necessary and label each stencil.

Using a utility knife, cut out each stencil. There should be nine stencils in all, including the birds, or six stencils if you decide to omit the birds.

3. Marking out the Surface
Using a pencil and ruler, mark points at least 10 inches down from the ceiling—more if you want extra white space above the pattern. Join the points with a light pencil line, checking that the line is level with a spirit level. Find and mark the center of each wall, which will be your starting point.

A detail of the stencilled flowers on the vine. *Photo by David Arky.*

On paper, roughly work out how many repeats of the design you will be able to fit on each wall. Because the birds are a conspicuous motif in the design, it is important to balance them. Experiment with the primary vine stencil before starting to paint, seeing how many times it will fit within one wall, and lightly mark the wall with pencil at the end of each repeat. You can easily adjust the spacing by stretching and shrinking the design between repeats. Then establish the positions of the flowers and the birds. Repeat for the remaining walls.

4. Applying the Stencils

Mix six separate saucers of the different colors of paint, thinning and tinting them to the desired consistency and colors. In this instance, a leaf green, a dull blue, an orange-red, a bright yellow, a grayish green, and a tan color were used. A tablespoonful of each mixed color, thinned, should be enough to complete the stencilling.

Following your plan for the repeats, first apply the vines and leaves, starting at the center of the first wall and working outward, continuing around corners and then right around the room. Register the stencil on previous outlines as you progress, and follow the pencil guideline on the wall. Stencil in the stems in grayish blue and the leaves in leaf green. Then stencil in the red and blue buds and the outer red parts of the flowers, leaving gaps for the birds where appropriate. Then stencil in the yellow inner parts of the flowers. Finally, stencil in the centers of the flowers, over the yellow inner parts.

Next, stencil in the birds, positioning two so that they face each other over the stem of the vine. First apply the main body in tan, then the tops of the wings, feet, beaks, and spikes on the head in blue, then the red parts of the feathers and the head decor, and finally the yellow feathers of the wings. With all the birds colored in, the stencilling is complete.

Two regal birds perch on the stem of the vine in place of the flowers and provide a focus to the design. *Photo by David Arky.*

The drawing below shows two complete repeats of the pattern.

Enlarge 325%

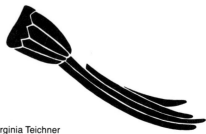

Stencils and designs © 1987 by Virginia Teichner

Enlarge elephant and horse 160%

Enlarge grass 260%

Enlarge all stencils 160%

This floorcloth, designed and painted by Kate Williams, demonstrates how traditional elements such as vines, hearts, and birds can be interpreted to give a lively and modern effect using nontraditional colors. A simple patchwork border executed in apricot and white lends a striking outline to the design. *Photo courtesy Kate Williams.*

Opposite page: A stencilled oval floorcloth by Lynn Goodpasture includes a background of *faux marbre*. The pattern is divided into a tile-like effect with the stencils trailing over the surface. *Photo by David Arky.*

CHAPTER SIX
Floorcloths

Colorfully painted floorcloths are one of the most charming results of the current revival of the art of stencilling. And yet to many of us the term *floorcloth* is unknown. A floorcloth consists of a piece of heavy-duty canvas that has been primed with paint on one side and decorated or stencilled with a pattern. Floorcloths are used in the home in place of a carpet or area rug to introduce color or decoration to an otherwise plain floor. After having been virtually obsolete for over a century in both America and Europe, they have become popular again because of the renewed interest in early American decorating techniques and because they complement the bare polished or painted wood floors featured in much of today's interior decoration.

Although floorcloths may be unfamiliar to many of us, they played an important role in both European and American homes in the eighteenth and nineteenth centuries. Many paintings of that time depict floorcloths in vivid colors and patterns as part of the background of interiors. Like their European forerunners, the earliest floor coverings in American homes were expanses of painted canvas, decorated with geometric de-

signs to simulate tiled floors, and stretching the width and length of a room. They served as an economical means of decorating otherwise stark and drafty wooden floorboards in the days when there were no manufactured carpets and floor coverings. In time, the patterns on the cloths became more elaborate and were filled with flowers and trellises executed in a variety of colors to echo more costly carpets and rugs.

Painted floorcloths were manufactured in large quantities in America from the mid-eighteenth century and were a standard furnishing in many a colonial home. As the patterns for floorcloths became more elaborate, stencilling them became popular because it was a much speedier, more economical means of execution. In time, also, the unwieldy, room-sized canvases were replaced by smaller cloths that could be moved from room to room.

Few early floorcloths survive because the paint and canvas disintegrated with time. But the current interest in American folk art and the prevailing taste for country-style decorating and for objects that are custom-made have combined to make the floorcloth a popular feature in many contemporary homes. The method of making floorcloths today remains simple and differs little from the days of their great vogue in Europe and colonial America.

Design Possibilities

Today the design possibilities for floorcloths are limitless. The effect you achieve will depend largely on the color combinations you choose and on whether you want to antique the surface after completing the stencilling or leave it clean and fresh. You can borrow from the earliest geometric patterns on floorcloths to create a simple yet lively effect. Alternating squares or diamonds, dogtooth triangle borders, checkerboard patterns, alternating stripes and stripe borders, and random geometric patterns painted in vivid contrasting colors all make attractive cloths.

Traditional flowers, birds, and vines translate well into floorcloth patterns too. Quilt designs and colors are an inexhaustible source of patterns and ideas. They contain a multitude of border patterns, single motifs, and pattern combinations that are especially suited to floorcloths. The proportions of a quilt are often similar to those of an average floorcloth, and so there is little need to scale the patterns up or down to achieve a balanced design. You might also explore the possiblities in Egyptian, Islamic, and Oriental designs, which can be used either as borders or as allover patterns executed in deep, rich colors.

As with most stencilling projects, you can also look around your home for pattern ideas. Ceramics, fabrics, and tiles provide a wealth of possibilities for coordinating a floorcloth with existing patterns in a room. Simple, naive patterns are some of the most effective. Children's motifs scattered in the center of a cloth and surrounded by a stripe border are extremely effective in a nursery or playroom. The animal stencil outlines featured in Chapter 5, arranged within a simple stripe border, would make a lively floorcloth.

Stencilled floorcloths also give you the opportunity to experiment with different painting techniques. You can blend colors within the stencil to achieve a shaded effect. You can sponge or glaze over the entire surface of backgrounds or only in designated areas. Rich, dark effects can be achieved by coating the surface with a gloss or semi-gloss varnish for depth of color. An antique effect can be produced by tinting the final varnish with a tiny quantity of raw umber artists' oil paint. Antiqued floorcloths work especially well on a natural wood floor because the grain of the wood complements the design.

Using a Stencilled Floorcloth

Although we have explored some of the history and design possibilities of handmade floorcloths, you may still be perplexed about how you might use one. The stiff, flat surface of the painted canvas does not fit the concept of using a carpet as cushioning on a floor. A painted canvas floorcloth, therefore, should not be considered simply as a substitute for a carpet or rug, in terms of either its practical or its decorative use on your floors. The rigid surface of a painted floorcloth, unlike the textured and pliable surface of a rug, will not give when bent. Consequently it is not advisable to place the cloth over a soft pile carpet, since any weight placed on the canvas may cause the surface to crack. The most appropriate use for a painted floorcloth is on a hard, supportive surface such as a wood or tile floor.

Consider also using a floorcloth to decorate a wooden deck or porch in the summer. Bright primary colors applied to the canvas in stripes or another simple pattern to coordinate with deck chairs and scatter cushions can create a stunning effect, and the canvas will provide a layer underfoot over the rougher wooden surface. Small-scale cloths can be made into table mats in exactly the same way, perhaps for use on outdoor tables. These require a lighter-weight canvas, but are primed and decorated in the same way as a floorcloth.

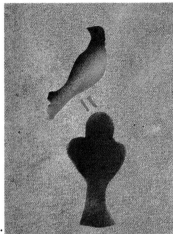

Details of various elements in the floorcloth pictured on page 100. The bird is delicately shaded using a mixture of paints within the stencil opening; the trailing vine separates out the central panel of the floorcloth.

The star pattern in the center is a traditional quilt motif. The detail at lower right is a good example of using a motif to turn a corner in a border design.

Materials and Techniques

The type of canvas used for a floorcloth is similar to the artists' canvas used in oil painting, and you will find it at awning stores or at sailcloth suppliers. Often known as duck canvas, it comes in a variety of weights or grades. For a floorcloth, no. 10 grade is best. It is durable and substantial and yet sufficiently pliable to bend for hemming or rolling. Duck canvas is made of natural cotton, in a creamy color, and generally is available in widths from 3 feet up to 9 feet. If you wish to make a particularly wide floorcloth, you can join pieces of canvas together using a flat seam sewn either by hand or by machine with sturdy needle and thread. When purchasing canvas, make sure it is chemically untreated. Transport your canvas home rolled, never folded. If necessary, you can steam iron it to eliminate creases.

MEASURING AND CUTTING THE CANVAS

Getting your canvas to the measurements you desire is a little tricky because the selvages, shrinkage, and the hem must all be accommodated. Canvas has a selvage running down each side, which must be removed before you start to measure out the size of your cloth. If you include it in your floorcloth, the tight weave of the selvage will distort the edges.

You will be priming the canvas with paint, which can cause it to shrink. When you cut your canvas to size, allow from 2 to 3 inches extra in the width and the length to accommodate shrinkage. It is difficult to say exactly how much the canvas will shrink, but usually an extra inch or so in the width or length of a finished floorcloth will not matter. Only when a floorcloth is to be fitted tightly into a space is the finished size critical; in this case, trim the canvas to size after priming.

You must also allow for a hem when measuring your canvas. Usually 1½ to 2 inches is adequate for a floorcloth.

Use chalk pencil, tailors' chalk, or soft pencil to mark the cutting lines on the raw canvas. These will brush off and in any case will be covered by layers of paint. Cut the canvas with sturdy, long-bladed scissors using clean, straight strokes. Or use a strong utility knife and a straightedge, but be sure not to damage the surface on which you are cutting.

PAINTING AND STENCILLING THE CANVAS

The first coat of your background color will serve as a priming coat and should be applied lightly but completely covering the canvas surface. Allow each coat of paint to dry thoroughly before applying the next. Your second coat will give you a good working surface on which to stencil. Background colors for a floorcloth should be flat latex paints or possibly flat oil-based paints. You should apply them evenly with a paintbrush or roller to achieve a good opaque surface. Save your background colors in case you make a mistake in stencilling and wish to paint it out. After you have finished your floorcloth, you can touch up little smudges with a small artists' brush and the background color.

If a design requires the elimination of all texture on the surface of the canvas, more layers of primer can be used. In this case, thin white latex paint with water to the consistency of heavy cream and apply two to three priming coats evenly to the canvas.

For stencilling a floorcloth, japan paints are ideal, but acrylics can also be used. If you use japan paints, you must wait two to three days before sealing the floorcloth.

FINISHING THE FLOORCLOTH

To hem the floorcloth, first trim the corners to get rid of excess canvas (see fig. 24). Then turn in the edges to make a hem and stick it down with a good craft glue or hot glue gun. The hem allowance may crack slightly as you turn it under. You can touch up the cracks with background paint once the glue has stuck.

To protect the surface of a floorcloth, apply two coats of flat or semi-gloss polyurethane varnish, which will make the surface relatively waterproof and allow you to sponge it lightly to clean. In time you may need to apply extra coats of varnish to protect the paintwork. The varnish can be tinted before application to give an antique effect.

SETTING UP A WORK SPACE

Before embarking on an ambitiously large project, you must first consider where you are going to make your floorcloth. Select the cloth's size and design to match your needs, expertise, and the area of work space available to you. If your work space is restricted to a kitchen table, then make your cloth slightly smaller than the tabletop. You can also work on the floor if you protect it with a substantial carpet of newspaper. Be sure there is sufficient room around the edge of the cut canvas to allow you to work all around. It is best to leave the cloth in place where you have painted it until it is dry; moving it single-handedly when wet is tricky, and you run the risk of smudging the paint and getting dust particles on the wet surface.

MAKING FLOORCLOTHS OF UNUSUAL SHAPES

Because you are starting with raw canvas that you cut to size yourself, you can make floorcloths in any shape or size you choose. Circular and oval floorcloths are very attractive placed in an open hallway or entrance. Measuring a circle can be tricky, but it can be done with a straight stick that measures half the diameter of the circle. Mark the center of the cloth and then move the stick around this point like a clock hand, marking points at the outer end of the stick. Then join the points and cut out the circle with scissors. To hem the cloth, draw another circle 1½ inches in from the edge with light chalk or pencil. Then snip inward to this circle from the edge, at 6-inch intervals all the way around the circle. Turn the edge under to the wrong side, following the chalk line and trimming away excess canvas to either side of the snips if necessary. Glue the hem in position in the usual way.

Octagonal and hexagonal floorcloths are also attractive and straightforward. Always remember to trim away excess canvas at corners or curves when you are hemming. You can even make a floorcloth to fit around a fixture in a room, such as a washbasin or a cupboard.

Caring for Your Floorcloth

If you need to move your floorcloth after it has been completed, roll it gently around a cardboard core after the varnish is thoroughly dry, with the stenciled surface to the inside. When you unroll it, loosen the roll and allow the cloth to relax gradually, rather than trying to make it lie flat at once, to prevent the varnish from cracking. In time, cracks may appear in the surface or the varnish may wear thin in places. Check it from time to time and apply a fresh coat of varnish when needed.

Kathie Marron-Wall's floorcloth design is simple and attractive. It is used here to decorate the floor of a girl's bedroom, breaking up the surface of the wooden floor. The colors were chosen to coordinate with other furnishings in the room and can be altered easily to suit different color schemes. *Photo by David Arky.*

project by
Kathie Marron-Wall

This floorcloth is one of the simplest projects in this book and is well within the capability of a newcomer to stencilling. Of manageable size, it can easily be executed in your home and does not require any special materials or equipment.

The floorcloth measures 3 feet by 4 feet and employs the standard decorative techniques of bordering, striping, and random pattern stencilling. The border, stripe, and central panel background can accommodate different patterns and colors— offering you the opportunity to adorn your floorcloth with any of the stencils you choose. The stencil pattern Kathie uses here is a simple rose motif that would be suitable for a living room, bathroom, landing, or bedroom. She has executed the pattern in shades of aqua, peach, and rose, but you can easily change the colors to fit any color scheme in your home.

If you prefer a less delicate pattern, almost any of the stencil outlines given in this book would be highly effective on a stencilled floorcloth, arranged within this simple border and stripe layout. Consider using the quilt patterns for the boxes in Chapter 4 or reducing the crisscross patterns given in Chapter 10. The vine in the wall pattern in Chapter 9 would make a very pretty edge on any floorcloth, with or without the medallion pattern placed in the center of the cloth.

DEGREE OF DIFFICULTY
Easy; suitable for a beginner

TIME REQUIRED
2½ days: cutting stencils and canvas, ½ day; applying background colors, ½ day; stencilling, 1 day; varnishing, ½ day; plus drying time

MATERIALS
basic equipment, page 12
2 sheets .004 Mylar® (10″ × 12″)
100% untreated no. 10 cotton duck canvas, 3′6″ x 4′6″ after
    selvages removed
strong dressmaking scissors
chalk pencil or soft-lead pencil

1 pt. flat latex paint (aqua)
1 pt. flat latex paint (peach)
3 flat paintbrushes (3″)
craft glue
rolling pin
thumbtacks (optional)
yardstick
2 stencil brushes (1″–1½″)
small jars
1 pt. semi-gloss polyurethane varnish

JAPAN COLORS
forest green
Prussian blue
dusty rose
burgundy
white

Note: The japan colors listed here are the ones Kathie used, which are Adele Bishop® brand. You can mix your own paints to match them, perhaps using artists' oils to tint your paints to the colors that you want. Remember that you can use raw umber or lamp black to darken colors.

1. Cutting and Painting the Canvas

Roll out the canvas on a clean, protected floor or table, ironing out any crease with a warm iron if necessary. Cut the selvages off the sides of the canvas.

Hold the canvas flat with thumbtacks or weights and draw a rectangle 3′6″ × 4′6″ in pencil or chalk on the surface, checking the corners with a right angle. Draw the lines of the rectangle as close to the grain of the canvas as possible. (Right-angled corners and a straight grain will help to ensure that your cloth lies as flat as possible.) Using clean, long strokes, cut the canvas along these lines. To store the canvas, always roll it up.

Apply one coat of peach latex paint over the entire surface to prime the canvas, using a clean brush or roller. Allow to dry thoroughly.

Measure the floorcloth again and trim it to measure 3′4″ × 4′4″, again checking that the corners are right angles. Then measure in 7½ inches from each side and mark points on the painted canvas surface with light conté pencil. Join up all the points with a straight pencil line to make a central rectangle. Place 1-inch-wide masking tape along the outside of this rectangle, making sure that the tape overlaps at the corners.

A detail of the flower stencil shows how paint was carefully blended to give the effect of two different shades of one color and how a single element of the rose design was isolated to occupy the inner corner.
Photo by David Arky.

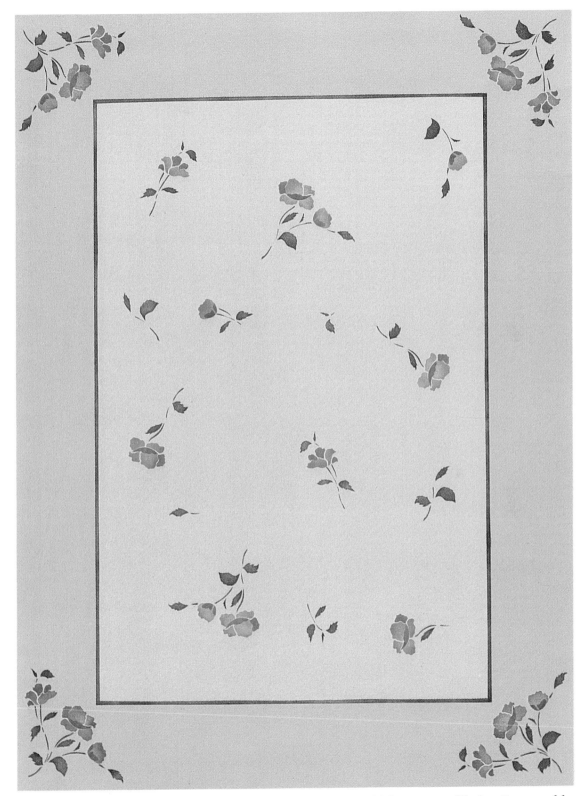

The background of the floorcloth is a basic layout against which any stencilled pattern could be applied. A plain colored border is separated from a central panel by a fine stripe. The flower pattern is then scattered haphazardly over the central panel. *Photo by David Arky.*

Using the peach latex paint again, add a second coat to this central panel, taking the paint up to, but not over, the masking tape. Allow the paint to dry and remove the masking tape.

Then place masking tape to the inside line of the central rectangle. Apply the aqua latex paint with a clean brush to the outside border. If the peach undercoat shows through, apply another coat of aqua to the border.

2. Cutting the Stencils

While you are waiting for the different coats of paint to dry, you can cut the stencils. Trace the outlines from this book onto tracing paper. There are three stencils in all. Cut pieces of Mylar® large enough for each stencil, allowing at least a 1-inch border all around. Then trace the outlines onto the frosted side with a drawing pen or permanent marker pen, making one stencil for each color and labeling it. To ensure proper placement of the flowers, trace the stems and leaves with dotted lines to use for registration. Cut out the stencil outlines, using the glass mat as a cutting surface.

3. Hemming the Canvas

When the floorcloth is thoroughly dry, mark points 2 inches in from the edge of the canvas all around. Join the points to make a line indicating the hem. Turn the floorcloth over onto a clean surface so that the painted surface is face down. Then turn in the hem all around to the underside of the canvas, using the edge of a ruler or yardstick if necessary to help you achieve a clean, straight fold. To avoid a lump of folded canvas at the corners, cut away a triangle of canvas to create a mitered corner (see fig. 25). Apply a good coating of craft glue to both sides of the hem down one side of the floorcloth. Press the hem firmly in place, using a rolling pin to distribute the glue evenly and form a flat join. Repeat for the remaining three sides, taking care not to leave loose threads at the corners. Touch up any places where the background paint has cracked.

4. Applying the Stencils

On your cookie sheet or tray, arrange the paper towels, saucers, teaspoons, palette knives, and turpentine. You will need to mix approximately 1 ounce of each color in a small jar. For the deep aqua blue, mix 3 parts forest green, ½ part Prussian blue, and 1 part white japan color. The rose color is 2 parts dusty rose, ¼ part burgundy, and ½ part white japan color. Thin each color with turpentine to the consistency of heavy

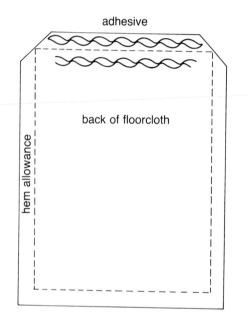

Figure 24 Hemming a floorcloth

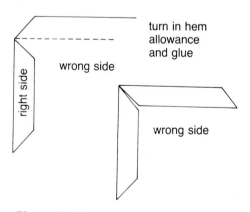

Figure 25 Turning in the corners

cream and transfer 2 teaspoons to a saucer.

Using a separate brush for each color, make proofs of the stencils on paper, taking care to have only a little paint on your brush. Paint in the entire stencil and then cut out the individual flowers. You will use them to establish the position of the stencils on the floorcloth. Using one of the proofs, work out the position of each rose in the corners of the aqua border.

Then position stencil 1 (the leaf stencil) in one corner to correspond with the proof position, aligning it so that there is about half an inch between the edge of the leaf outline and the edge of the floorcloth. Using the dark aqua paint, stencil in the leaf print. Repeat for the other three corners. Then take stencil 2, and using your registration marks, place it over the leaves. Use the rose paint, but apply it lightly to achieve a paler shade than the stencil to follow. Repeat for the other three corners. Then print in stencil 3, using several applications of paint to achieve a darker color of rose. Vary the intensity of color within the stencils for a shaded effect.

There is no distinct pattern for the flowers in the central peach panel. Again using the paper proofs, flop the stencil outlines to make flowers bend in the opposite direction and use portions of the flowers for a varied effect. When you have roughly worked out your design, lightly fix the proofs in position with masking tape. Then stencil in the outlines onto the center of the floorcloth to correspond with the proofs. If your design involves flopping the stencil, make sure that the reverse side is clean of paint before you turn the stencil over.

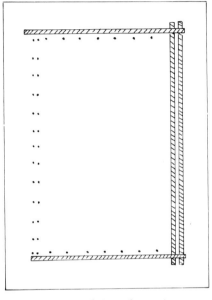

Figure 26 Applying the stripe to the floorcloth

5. Applying the Stripe

Measure 5¾ inches in from the turned-in edges of the floorcloth all around and mark points with light pencil or chalk. (Only mark close to the central peach panel and not in the aqua border.) Join the lines together around the center panel and place strips of 1-inch masking tape to the inside of this line. Then measure ½ inch out from the masking tape edge and again draw lines all around. Place masking tape to the outside of this line so that you have a ½-inch stripe where the aqua and peach areas meet.

Using dark aqua, paint in this stripe, taking care not to smudge the paint over the masking tape. Apply a second coat if necessary. Remove the tape on both sides to reveal the stripe.

6. Finishing Off

Leave the floorcloth to dry for about three days. Then apply three coats of semi-gloss polyurethane varnish to the painted surface, allowing each coat to dry before applying the next.

Use same size

Sample print

A chest of drawers creatively stencilled by Mary MacCarthy with delicate wildflower forms. *Courtesy* The World of Interiors *(U.K.). Photo by James Mortimer.*

Opposite page: A detail of the stencilled designs on Mary MacCarthy's kitchen dresser, which is pictured on page 146. *Photo by John Vere Brown.*

CHAPTER SEVEN
Furniture

The current resurgence of interest in painted finishes on furniture, such as glazing, lacquering, staining, and marbling, has brought about a renewed interest in the art of stencilling furniture. In many ways the stencilling of furniture stands apart from other stencilling techniques. Whether produced today or in past ages, it has an effect that is much more sophisticated than the simple outlines and patterns created in wall and floor stencilling. It requires a greater sympathy between the form of the stencil and the form of the piece of furniture, and the craftsman must also be skilled in preparing and working with wooden surfaces.

Almost all countries at some time have experienced a vogue for painted and decorated furniture. In Japan, centuries-old traditions of lacquering and painting furniture have brought about the finest surfaces imaginable. In Asia, from India to Russia, a propensity for rich, pure colors ornamented with gilt has produced a heritage of unique and charming furniture. In Europe, painted furniture has always been a part of the folk craft. Scandinavian tradition prefers the soft faded colors of nature—greens and blues subtly accented with colored impressions of flowers and other natural motifs.

The colors of Austria and Bavaria are characteristically rich, with deep reds, greens, and blues forming a background to simple forms elaborately executed in gold, black, umber, and yellow. In France, in addition to the lavish gilt-laden armoires and commodes of the eighteenth century, there are the delicate painted pieces of Provence, which echo the vivid palette of the countryside. In England in medieval times, painted screens and furniture executed in the purest, richest colors were used to adorn churches. William Morris and others in the Arts and Crafts movement in late-nineteenth-century England revived the taste for richly painted furniture influenced by medieval and gothic themes.

Settlers in America brought with them an appreciation of painted furniture and devised methods of decorating furniture that became distinctively American. The clear colors and primitive decorative skills seen in Pennsylvania Dutch furniture evoke the furniture of their Bavarian and Austrian forerunners. These unsophisticated pieces of furniture from the late eighteenth century glowed with the pure bright colors in which they were executed. Reds, yellows, greens, and browns were the characteristic palette of these often somber people, whose un-abashed artistry contrasted strangely with their reserved demeanor. Of all their pieces of furniture, it is perhaps the wonderful dower chests, decorated in a skillful combination of freehand painting and stencilling, that are most familiar to us.

One of the best-known examples of stencilled furniture in America is the Hitchcock chair. An elegant, small chair with a dark stained-wood or black-painted surface and delicate gilt stencilling, it has been a staple of many an American home for well over a century. The stencilling is characterized by the use of bronzing powders, which produce subtly shaded effects within the stencilled outlines. The bronzing powder is applied through delicate stencils to a surface that has been treated with sizing compound, which is an adhesive that holds the grains of pigment. We attribute the Hitchcock chair to one Lambert Hitchcock, from Hitchcocksville, Connecticut, who in the late 1820s set up a thriving workshop where the chairs were produced. Many artisans went on to duplicate these chairs, which filled a gap in homes that could not afford expensive mahogany and walnut occasional chairs. This style of furniture decoration, which simulates more elaborate lacquer methods is still important in furniture stencilling today.

Stencilling on furniture tends to be most successful when the surface of the wood has been treated, since outlines sometimes lose their clarity when stencilled directly onto raw wood. There are a number of ways to treat the wood—by glazing, staining, japanning, and gessoing, to name but a few. If you are interested in learning how to apply one of these finishes to your piece of furniture, consult one of the comprehensive books available on the subject, such as *Paint Magic* by Jocasta Innes (New York, Van Nostrand Reinhold; London, Frances Lincoln Publishers, 1981). Glazing or staining will produce a much softer effect than a coat of paint, which simply lies on the surface and gives no depth of color. However, if you do use a painted background, you can add depth by applying a coat of tinted semigloss varnish when the stencilling is complete.

Many pieces of furniture respond well to stencilling, and the type of stencil you choose and the final effect you achieve will depend on

An early painted Pennsylvania Dutch dower chest. *Courtesy The Metropolitan Museum of Art, Rogers Fund, 1923 (23.16).*

furniture that will benefit from painting and stencilling. Valuable antique pieces should be left untouched because stencilling and painting will detract from their value as well as their aesthetic qualities. The extent to which you stencil a piece of furniture will depend on the form of the piece, but generally it is best to limit stencilling to specific areas rather than use an overall pattern that might overwhelm the shape of the piece. Stencilling can also be used to introduce shapes into a flat furniture surface, as in Lynn Goodpasture's project in this chapter.

When you are considering stencilling a piece of furniture, take a good look at it and note the shapes and forms of its various parts. Shaped chair backs, turned legs, moldings, and shaped tabletops will all influence the type of stencils you choose to decorate the piece with. Your stencils should conform to the shape and proportions of the piece of furniture. For example, a chair back might have two cross-supports that are curved and shaped in a particular way. Select stencils that fit in with and complement these curves so that they enhance the shape of the chair rather than detract from it. Take into account the symmetry of a piece of furniture and align your stencil along the central axis if necessary, with the remainder of the pattern falling evenly to either side. You will find it difficult to apply flat stencils to curved and turned legs; freehand painting is much simpler and more effective. If you do want to rely on stencils, use a design with very small cutouts that do not have to be bent with the curvature of the surface.

A Hitchcock chair delicately decorated with bronze stencils. *Courtesy The Hitchcock Chair Company, Riverton, Connecticut.*

the shape and age of the piece. The best pieces of furniture to stencil are those that are bought inexpensively—secondhand or new, unfinished

Lynn Goodpasture's design for a pine blanket chest. The pattern is based on traditional
Pennsylvania Dutch themes and motifs from Egyptian art and employs a variety of paint finishes
on the wood surface. *Photo by David Arky.*

This project comprises a simple blanket chest or dower chest. The rectangular box was handmade in pine by a Connecticut craftsman, Ian Ingersoll, especially for this project. However, such boxes are readily available, both new and old, and the pattern illustrated has been designed so that you can adapt it to the proportions of any similar box you come across. Some blanket chests stand on feet at each corner, but this one rests directly on the floor. If your chest does have feet, you can easily adapt part of the pattern or devise your own pattern to decorate them. If the chest is already painted or coated with varnish, it must be thoroughly stripped to its natural wood. You can do this yourself with paint stripper or have a professional dip the chest in caustic solution.

Lynn Goodpasture decorated this chest with a delicate combination of paint finish and stencilling. The effect is one of lightness and airiness that counteracts the solidity of the chest itself. Lynn began by spreading cherry stain thinly over the untreated pine surface to add depth to the base color and then applied a superficial layer of white glaze over the cherry stain. The cherry stain gives the white glaze a floating effect and at the same time enhances the handcrafted features of the box—the dovetail joints, the simple routed edge, and the pretty grain of the wood. If she had used a simple coat of flat white paint in place of the stain and glaze, the box would have sat heavily and the stencilling would have shouted against the solid background. Instead, the staining and glazing set the translucent tone of the entire piece.

The glazing mixture consists of flatting oil and glaze coat, which are available from hardware and art-supply stores. Lynn combines this mixture with a small proportion of flat or eggshell finish oil-based paint, which for this project was white. You can mix the base with any color of oil-based paint you prefer for a glaze that can be used with or without stencilling.

The stencil pattern derives from several sources. The fantail outlines spanning the fronts and sides are Egyptian inspired, both in shape and color. The arch-like pattern dictating the layout of the remaining stencils owes its origins to the Pennsylvania Dutch. Many of their dower chests were deco-

rated across the front with a sequence of two or three arches that contained a variety of emblems and motifs. Here there are four arches, and around the base is a version of the sawtooth border popular in much folk art.

Lynn chose the color scheme as a contrast to the traditional inspiration of the pattern. To emphasize the lightness of the chest, she used a combination of hot and cold colors, which work against each other, thereby introducing movement into the design. Cool blues and warm blues, lilacs and greens, reds and yellows make up her palette, which produces an effect that is both brilliant and subtle. Within each arch she has blended warm and cool grays to give a cloud-like effect over the surface.

If these colors do not fit any of your decorating schemes, you can easily change them to create a piece of furniture with a very different character. By replacing the light background with a dark solid color such as deep red, charcoal gray, or dark green, you would add weight to the chest, which would not require the delicate mottling of the surface between the arches. Flower stems and centers could be applied in gold paint for a rich antique effect. The dentil border could be applied in black, dark red, or dark green over the base color to add depth to the chest at the base. Look at old chests or pictures of old chests in books about American folk decoration to find examples of traditional color schemes and decorative effects.

Adapting the pattern to a chest of different proportions is easy. The box used in this project measures 19½ inches wide by 41 inches long by 18½ inches high, but small deviations from these measurements can be easily accommodated. Because there is a definite back to the box, any slightly uneven joins in the border can fall there and not detract from the main pattern. The height of the sawtooth pattern must be adapted to fit into the depth of the base of the box you are using, but if you start in the exact center of the front and work your way around to the back evenly to either side of this center point, your pattern will always balance at each corner. Join the two ends of the border in the best-looking way you can, perhaps leaving room to include a signature or small motif if the space is larger than one element of the pattern but not large enough for two (see photograph at left).

The arches across the front and on each side also can be stretched or shrunk to fit any similar size of chest. This is explained more fully in the step-by-step instructions for the project. Any adjustments in these proportions will also take care of the distribution of the flower decorations.

The decoration of the lid is based on a sequence of three rectangles that correspond with the dimensions of the lid itself.

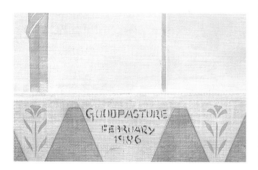

GOODPASTURE
FEBRUARY
1986

When modifying the sawtooth border pattern to fit the dimensions of the chest, Lynn came up with a simple solution by including space for her signature. *Photo by David Arky.*

If your lid is smaller, narrower, or wider, you will need to adjust the rectangles accordingly. If you wish to decorate a box of considerably smaller dimensions, work out proportionately how much it differs and reduce the size of the stencils accordingly.

The painting technique involved in decorating the chest requires not only stencilling but also masking. Masking entails using a piece of acetate cut to a specific shape to cover certain areas while paint is being applied to adjacent sections. This technique was used to apply paint to the areas within the arches.

To finish the chest, Lynn applied three coats of flat varnish to all the sides. She does not use a polyurethane varnish because she prefers a more refined surface for furniture, but you can decide either way. Before application Lynn cut the varnish by mixing it with solvent to achieve a thinner coat and a less yellow veil over the existing paintwork. Three parts of varnish to one part of solvent were used here. The interior of the box was painted with colored glazes to complement the pattern on the outside.

To paint and stencil the chest, you will need to set aside a space where it can stand while you are working. You need to be able to work all around it, and the room should be well ventilated and free of dust. Because the stencilling reaches right to the bottom edge of the chest, you might want to rest it on supports—for example, two stools—so that this edge is free on all sides. Raising the chest up in this way also allows you to work without having to bend down constantly. Use a stick of

Figure 27 Dimensions of the chest

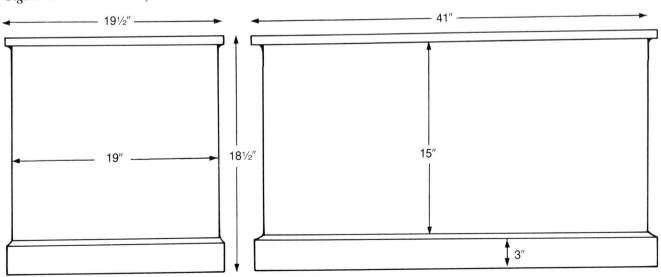

wood to prop open the lid while you work so that you can paint right up to the edges.

DEGREE OF DIFFICULTY Advanced. This is an involved project, requiring skill in fitting stencils to a chest that might not be the same size, and adeptness in combining a variety of stencils. It also entails various painting techniques. For these reasons, it really should not be undertaken by a beginner.

TIME REQUIRED Several days or longer, depending on the skill of the stenciller.

MATERIALS
basic equipment, page 12
4 sheets .0075 acetate
scissors
sandpaper (medium and fine)
tack cloth
cheesecloth
cherry stain
flat paintbrush (2")
½ pt. flatting oil
½ pt. glaze coat
½ pt. eggshell or flat oil-based paint (white)
small jars
turpentine
9 stencil brushes (1–1½")
artists' oil paint (cobalt violet)
small can bronzing powder (silver)
gold sizing compound
artists' paintbrush (¼")
eggshell furniture varnish
paintbrush or sponge brush (2")
mineral spirits

JAPAN COLORS
Prussian blue
ultramarine blue
striping white
raw umber
lamp black
emerald green
CP green medium
liberty red
signcraft red
chrome yellow light

1. Preparing the Background

Sand the wood surface of the box wherever necessary to make it completely smooth. Wipe with a tack cloth to remove all dust particles.

Using a piece of cheesecloth, wipe the cherry stain lightly over the surface of the chest, following the wood grain. Allow the stain to sink into the wood for 10 minutes and then wipe off the excess with a clean piece of cheesecloth. Leave the stain to dry overnight. Apply the stain to the outside of the chest only.

Make the glaze base by measuring equal amounts of flatting oil and glaze coat into a coffee can or jar and mixing thoroughly. Then add white paint—one part paint to three parts glaze base—to make the white glaze medium. Mix thoroughly and apply with a 2-inch paintbrush to the stained surface. Brush on with long, light strokes, taking care that the glaze does not build up or drip at the edges and corners. Place a support inside the lid of the chest so that you can glaze right up to the edges of both the box and the lid. The glaze will take on a slightly streaky appearance because of the cherry stain underneath. This will add texture to your stencilling, but make sure that the grain of the wood does not show through too noticeably. One coat of glaze should suffice.

2. Making the Stencils

Trace the stencil outlines, reducing or enlarging them as necessary to fit the size of your chest. (See step 6 for adapting the arch patterns to a different-sized chest. It is not always necessary to change the proportions of the stencils; in most instances they can simply be shortened or extended.)

Cut pieces of acetate large enough for each stencil, allowing at least 2 inches extra all around for a border. Trace the outlines onto the acetate using permanent ink and label each stencil as you finish.

Using the glass cutting mat and the utility knife, cut out all the stencils except the arch stencils, which you will find best to cut when you need them. You should have seventeen stencils in all.

3. Mixing the Paints

Mix the paints for each stencil. Because the quantities of paint are so small, you can mix as you need them, but the recipes and approximate quantities are as follows:

Warm blue Prussian blue, 1 part; ultramarine blue, ¾ part; striping white, 2 parts; raw umber, ¼ part; lamp black, ¼ part. Quantity: 2 teaspoons.

Cool green Prussian blue, ½ part; ultramarine blue, 1 part; striping white, 3 parts; raw umber, ¼ part; lamp black, ¼ part; emerald green, 1 part. Quantity: 2 teaspoons.

Warm green CP green medium, 1 part; striping white, 1½ parts. Quantity: 2 teaspoons.

Cool blue Ultramarine blue, 1 part; striping white, 1 part; lamp black, ¼ part; warm blue mixture, dash. Quantity: 3 teaspoons.

Lavender Cobalt violet, 1 part; striping white, 1 part; cool blue mixture, ½ part. Quantity: 3 teaspoons. (Cobalt violet is a fast-drying artists' oil paint and can therefore be used in a larger proportion.)

Cool pale gray Lavender mixture, ¼ part; striping white, 3 parts; lamp black, ½ part. Quantity: 1½ tablespoons.

Warm pale gray Striping white, 3 parts; raw umber, ½ part. Quantity: 1½ tablespoons.

Red Liberty red medium, 1 part; signcraft red, 1 part; striping white, 2 parts; emerald green, ¼ part. Quantity: 2 teaspoons.

Yellow Chrome yellow light, 2 parts; striping white, 1 part. Quantity: 2 teaspoons.

4. Stencilling the Lower Border

The same stencil is used for the blue and green areas of the zigzag border (stencil 1). Find and mark the center of the base of the chest. Align the center of the zigzag stencil with the center of the base and hold in place with masking tape.

Figure 28 Marking out positions for the flowers and stems across the front, back, and side panels

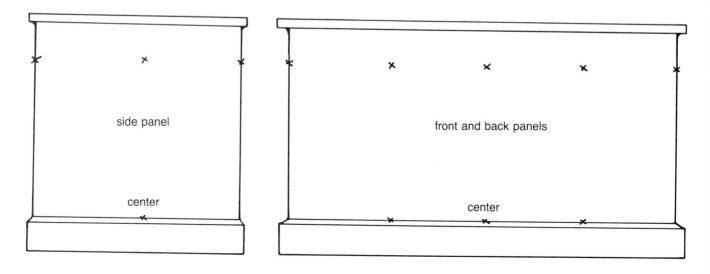

Using warm blue paint, apply the blue part of the border, working to either side of the center mark and registering the stencil on previously stencilled prints. Continue until the two ends of the border meet at the back (adjust the pattern accordingly).

Clean the stencil and turn it upside down. Fill in the tops of the zigzags with cool green paint, again working to either side of the center mark and meeting at the back.

Flower border Position the flower border (stencil 2) over each of the blue teeth of the border and stencil in these outlines in warm green, working all the way around the base of the box.

5. Stencilling the Stems and Flowers on the Sides of the Chest

Find the center of the front panel and lightly mark it in pencil at the bottom edge. It should correspond with the center of the base border. Then find and mark the centers of each half so formed. Treat the back of the chest in exactly the same way. Now find and mark the center of one side panel. Repeat for the other side panel. Using a ruler and a right angle to ensure the lines are vertical, make light pencil dashes at points approximately 12 inches above the first pencil marks around the bottom (see fig. 28).

At each of these points, stencil in the stems of the fan-shaped flowers (stencil 3) in warm green paint, using the pencil marks as a guide and to ensure that the stems are vertical. Stencil in the stems on the front, sides, and back panels. Then stencil in the red fan-shaped flowers (stencil 4) on each of these stems using red paint. One stem and one red flower will fall at each corner. Tape the stencil to the front of the chest so that only half of it will print and the remainder will stand out in space. Mask out the adjacent side with a strip of masking tape. Stencil in this half of the outline, both the green stem and the red flower, and allow the paint to dry thoroughly (see fig. 29). Lift the masking tape from the adjacent side of the corner and mask the stencilled half in the same way. Apply the other half of the stencil to the remaining side of the corner to complete the flower and stem.

6. Stencilling the Arches on the Sides

The arches are the one part of this design that will need to be adapted if your chest is a slightly different length from the one used here. Find the midpoints between each of the green stems. If the distance between one stem and one midpoint is 5 inches, the arch stencils (stencils 5 and 6) will fit

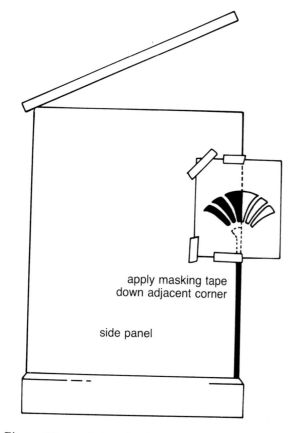

apply masking tape
down adjacent corner

side panel

Figure 29 Applying the flower stencil around a corner

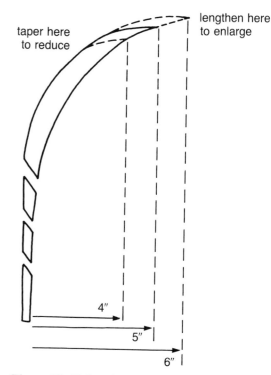

taper here
to reduce

lengthen here
to enlarge

4"

5"

6"

Figure 30 Enlarging or reducing the arch stencil

without alteration. In this case simply trace and cut each stencil in the usual way.

If the interval measures *more* than 5 inches, then the arches must be extended when you apply them. To do this, cut a piece of acetate large enough to accommodate the scaled-up stencil and the extension (plus a 2-inch border). Trace the arch onto the acetate as you would normally, but continue the line of the arch as required for it to reach the edge of the fan flower (see fig. 30). Then cut out the stencil.

If the interval is *smaller* than 5 inches, you will need to mask out the end of the curve of the arch so it doesn't overlap the flower. To do this, cut the stencil to the normal size, but also cut a piece of acetate to mask the flower exactly (see fig. 31). When you come to stencil in the arches, hold the mask over the flower with masking tape so that no paint smudges over into the stencilled flower. This shortening and extending will work only for discrepancies of about 1 to 3 inches. For greater discrepancies, the entire arch must be scaled up or down.

Applying the arches The arches are made from two half-arch stencils. The entwining stems (stencil 7) around the arches alternate in direction across the surface of the chest. The two

stencils are applied so that the entwining stem bends one way first, but then the stencils are cleaned, turned over, and applied so that the stem bends the other way on the next arch. Each side of the arch should be positioned to either side of the pencil ticks along the bottom edge.

Within the pattern the colors of the arches alternate, as do the colors of the twining stems binding the stems of the arches. Working from the left, paint the first and third arches in warm blue and the second and fourth arches in lavender. Continue alternating these forms and colors right around the chest. To do this, print all the warm blue arches first, starting at the front left-hand corner and working around the sides and back. Then print in the lavender arches in the remaining space.

With these in position, take stencil 7 and fill in the twining stems around each arch, using lavender paint with the warm blue arches and warm green with the lavender arches. Alternate the direction of the wrapping stems with the different colors to correspond with the direction dictated by the gaps in the arches.

Next stencil in the flower petals that sit on the warm green flower centers between two arches. First apply the small inner petals (stencils 8 and 9) in yellow and then the bigger outer petals (stencils 10 and 11) in red.

To apply the gray shaded areas between the arches, use the arch stencil to cut a piece of acetate that masks the arch and leaves the area within it exposed (see fig. 32). Then blend very light coats of the warm and cool gray paints within these areas, all around the sides of the chest.

The pattern spanning the front of the chest. The arches can be widened or narrowed to fit different dimensions and the flowers fitted in between as shown here. *Photo by David Arky.*

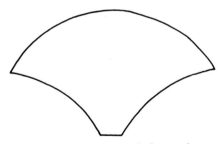

Figure 32 Acetate mask for arch

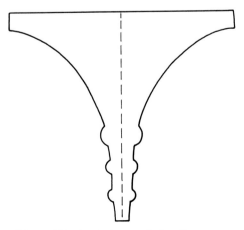

Figure 31 Acetate mask for flower

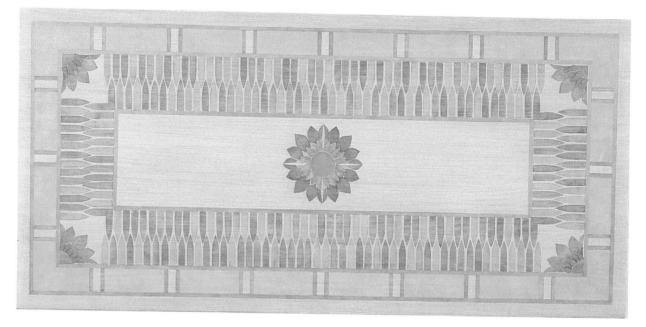

The stencilled pattern on the lid. Three concentric rectangles painted in silver contain the various elements of the design. The tooth-like outlines meet at right angles in each corner. The double stripes pick up the colors of the pattern on the front, and between each double stripe is a panel of shaded paint that repeats the treatment between the arches on the front. The central flower is formed by aligning the four quarter segments.
Photo by David Arky.

7. Decorating the Lid

The pattern on the lid can readily be adapted to different dimensions. Measure points 1 inch in from the edge of the lid all around and mark with pencil dots. Join the dots to form a rectangle. Then measure points 2 inches in from this rectangle and again join them to form a second rectangle within the first. Find and mark the midpoints of each side of the two rectangles.

Applying the border pattern A colored tooth border (stencil 12) is applied to the inside of the inner rectangle. Lynn decided to stencil the first teeth of the border in warm blue, and then used these first prints to register the following colors. Start at the center of one end and work out toward one corner. When you reach the corner, use the corner stencil (stencil 13) to turn at a right angle so that two blue teeth are at each side of the corner at right angles to each other (see photograph). Then proceed all the way around, treating each corner in the same way. When you complete the warm blue prints, clean the stencil and then fill in the remaining teeth, applying cool blue, warm green, and lavender in a random manner and using existing teeth as a register. Clean the stencil each time you introduce a new color.

Applying the silver stripes Use the two marked-out rectangles as the outer borders of each of the two outermost stripes. Then mark points ¼ inch in from the outer rectangle and ¼ inch in from the inner rectangle as a guide for the width of the stripe. Join the points around each rectangle with a light pencil line to form two parallel stripes ¼ inch wide with a space 1½ inches wide in between. Mask to either side of each stripe with strips of acetate. Then mark and mask off another ¼-inch stripe just within the tooth border in the same way.

To make the silver paint, mix 1 tablespoon of gold sizing compound with 1 tablespoon of the silver bronzing powder. Using a ¼-inch artists' paintbrush, apply the paint between the masking tape on each of the three stripes. Allow it to dry and then apply a second coat. Allow this to dry thoroughly overnight before stencilling further.

Corner flowers Using the corner flower center (stencil 14), apply the warm green flower centers in each corner. Then use stencils 8 and 9 to apply the inner red petals, and finally stencils 10 and 11 to apply the outer yellow petals.

Central flower Using a yardstick, find the center of the innermost rectangle by measuring in from each midpoint on the sides of the lid. Mark the center with a cross in light pencil. Align the complete flower center (stencil 15) with the center, and print in the warm green center. Then use the inner petal stencils (8 and 9) to print the inner yellow petals, aligning the stencils around the center to complete the flower. Finally use stencils 10 and 11 to add the outer red petals.

Lid border Find the midpoint on all four sides again and mark the midpoints between the two outermost silver lines on each side. Using the stripe border stencil (stencil 16), print in double lines in warm green on each center mark so that the two lines fall evenly to each side of it. With these center lines in position, the remaining lines in the border correspond to the colors and positions of the pattern on the front of the chest— that is, each pair of green lines falls directly over all the flowers with green stems; the lavender lines fall directly over all the lavender arches; and the cool blue lines fall over all the cool blue arches (see photograph). This means that the spacing of the lines within the silver stripes will correspond with the spacing of the arches and flowers across the front, back, and sides of the chest. In the case of Lynn's chest, this interval was 5 inches. Adjust yours accordingly and mark the positions of the stripes on the lid between the silver lines.

Use the long rectangle stencil (stencil 17) to fill in the areas between each of the pairs of stripes. These are painted in the same way as the areas under the arches on the front, using spots of warm gray and cool gray and blending the edges to produce a soft, mottled effect. The small rectangle between one pair of colored lines has been left unstencilled with just the background showing through to contrast with the mottled rec-

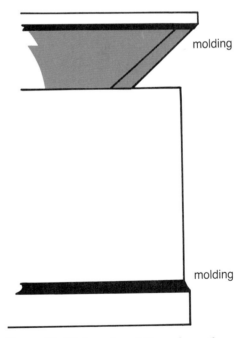

Figure 34 Strips of molding along the bottom of the lid and around the base

tangles, so be sure your paint is strong enough to make this contrast evident.

With a fine ¼-inch paintbrush, paint the molded strip around the bottom of the lid in any of the colors previously used, to form a contrasting stripe around the lid. Prop open the lid to paint this strip, and do not close it until the paint is thoroughly dry. If there is a similar molded strip around the stand of the base, paint this in the same way.

8. Finishing Off

Allow the paint work on the chest to dry for four days, longer if the weather is particularly humid. Make sure the silver areas are completely dry. Wipe over the entire surface with a tack cloth and then prop the lid open with a stick. Use good-quality furniture varnish and cut it with 1 part mineral spirits to 3 parts varnish. Mix the mineral spirits and varnish well and then apply to all the painted surfaces using a 2-inch paintbrush or disposable sponge brush. As you apply the varnish, take into account the direction of the wood grain; brush with horizontal strokes across the lower base and with vertical strokes over the sides. This prevents the varnish from dripping and causing an effect known as veiling. Allow it to dry thoroughly and then varnish the lid, using the same horizontal strokes as

Figure 33 Plan for stencilling the lid

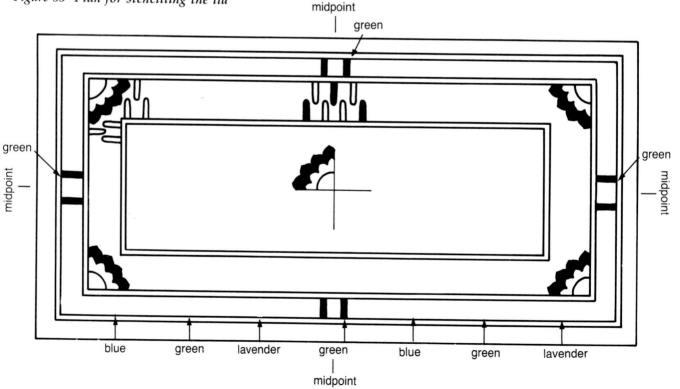

for the lower base for both the top of the lid and the lower edge of the lid.

After each coat of varnish, inspect for any drips, which must be brushed out while the varnish is still wet. When each coat is dry, wipe the surface with a tack cloth before applying the next coat. The chest will need two to five coats of varnish, depending on how and where it will be used. To bring out the shine of the silver bronzing powder, you might want to paint a strip of gloss varnish over the silver stripes after the previous varnishing is finished.

Finishing the inside of the chest How you finish the inside is a matter of choice, but a painted interior lends an interesting touch to the chest. Lynn chose to paint the inside of the base with a pale blue wash, and the inside of the lid with a pale green wash. To do this, she painted the entire interior surface with white primer and then one coat of flat white oil-based paint. She then applied a thin wash of pale blue, painted in one direction to produce a grain effect. When this had dried, she applied the same blue wash in the opposite direction to produce an almost woven effect of crossing grains. She painted the inside of the lid with pale green wash in the same way. For extra protection, she applied two coats of varnish.

Caring for the chest The varnished surface of the chest can be wiped with a damp sponge to remove any dirt. Avoid using oil or wax polishes in case you later wish to touch up the surface of the varnish or paint work. Keep an eye on the corners for wear and apply extra varnish if they appear to be chipping or wearing thin.

A pale blue glaze applied over a white surface gives a streaked effect inside the chest. *Photo by David Arky.*

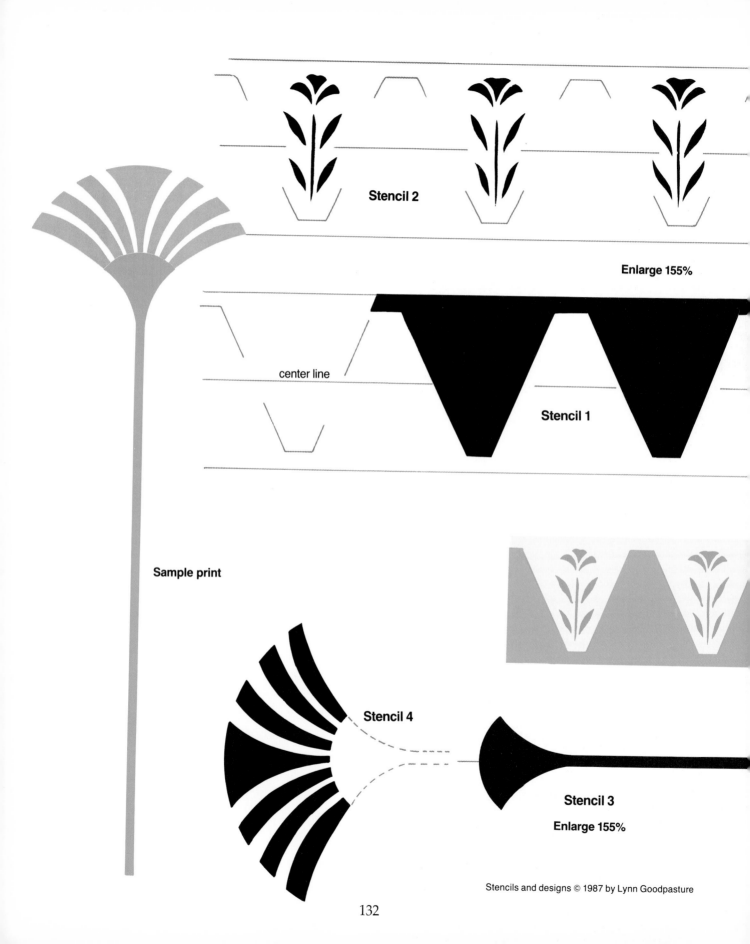

Stencil 2

Enlarge 155%

center line

Stencil 1

Sample print

Stencil 4

Stencil 3

Enlarge 155%

Stencils and designs © 1987 by Lynn Goodpasture

132

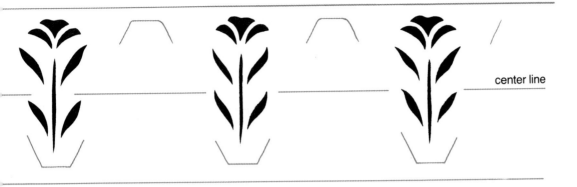

center line

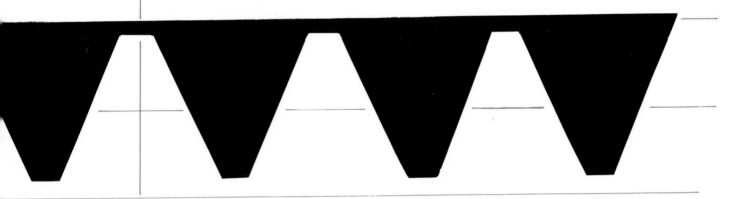

center line

Sample print

base line   center line

133

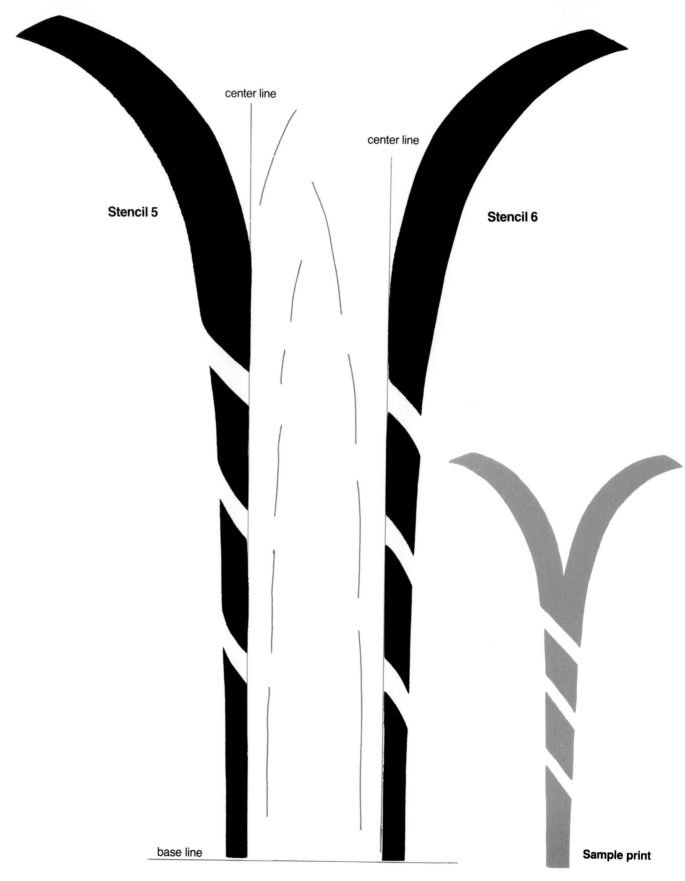

center line

center line

Stencil 5

Stencil 6

base line

Sample print

134

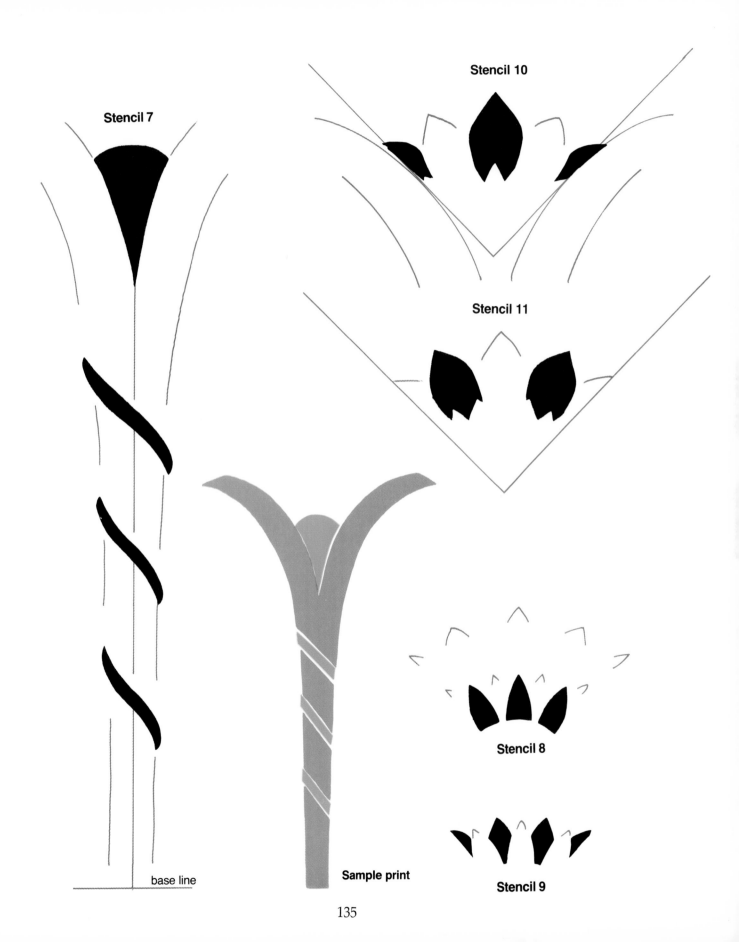

Stencil 7

Stencil 10

Stencil 11

Stencil 8

Stencil 9

base line

Sample print

135

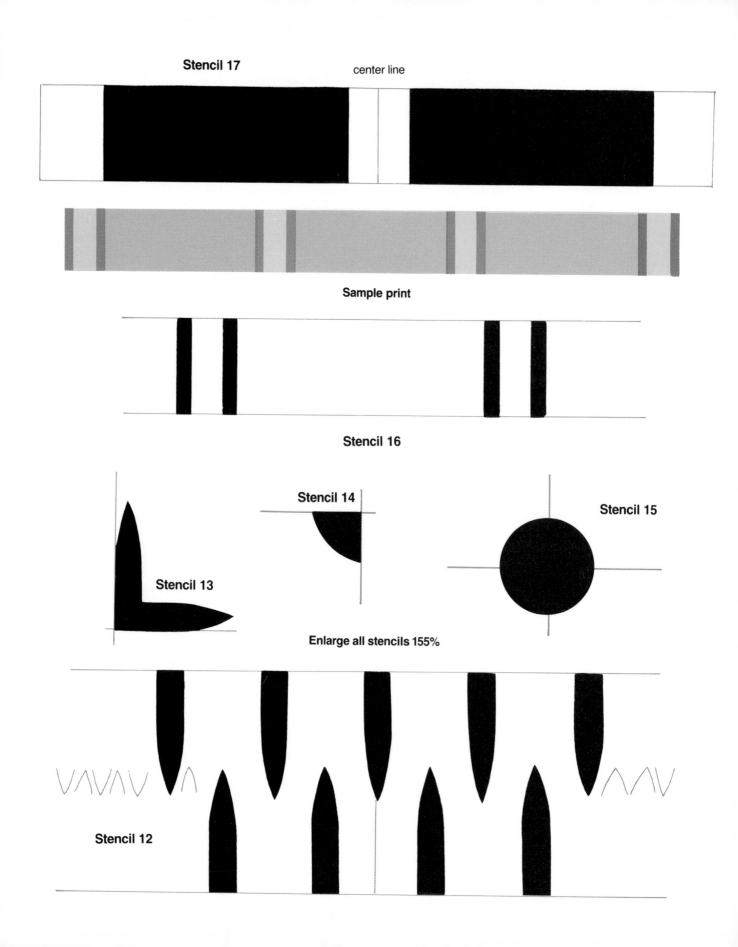

Stencil 17

center line

Sample print

Stencil 16

Stencil 14

Stencil 15

Stencil 13

Enlarge all stencils 155%

Stencil 12

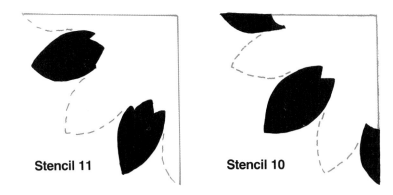

Stencil 11   **Stencil 10**   **Stencil 9**   **Stencil 8**

Stencils 8, 9, 10, 11 shown here for reference only.

Sample print

Sample print

An early American stencilled bedcovering. *Courtesy the Museum of American Folk Art, New York.*

Opposite page: Karen Meister stencilled the pattern in the center of this pillow using an Adele Bishop® precut stencil and then mounted it with printed fabric.
Courtesy Adele Bishop Inc.

138

CHAPTER EIGHT

Textiles

Although many people regard stencilling on fabric as a recent development, it in fact dates back to the early nineteenth century. We have already encountered it in the form of stencilled floorcloths, and around the time when stencilled floorcloths were flourishing there was a similar vogue for stencilled counterpanes, stencilled bed hangings, and stencilled window blinds.

One early example of stencilled textiles is the bedcover featured opposite, which demonstrates extraordinarily deft brush and paint work and surpasses many of the examples of fabric stencilling we see today. Stencilling bedcovers, tablecloths, and scarves was a popular folk art around 1820 in America and occupied much the same role in women's lives as patchwork and appliqué quilting. Delicate, brightly colored designs were applied to undyed homespun cotton, which was usually left unbacked and unquilted and used for summer bed coverings or tablecloths. Sometimes the stencilled patterns would be combined with freehand painting, and generally the patterns would be floral in inspiration. At the height of their popularity, stencilled bed coverings took the place of costly embroidered bed coverings in more humble homes, and not

surprisingly the patterns were designed in imitation of their more luxurious counterparts.

Many early stencilled textiles used a palette taken from theorem paintings, which were also very popular at this time. Bowls of fruits and flowers were the subject matter of these small, framed stencilled paintings, which were often executed on velvet backgrounds. The same greens, reds, yellows, and blues that theorem painters used were picked up by stencillers to create patterns of great beauty.

At first, homemakers themselves traced and cut the stencils for the designs, which imitated rare printed textiles. Later, around 1835, mass-produced commercial stencil patterns became available and simplified their task. The stencils were attached to the fabric, and cotton balls soaked in dye were dabbed through the stencil openings. These dyes did not perform in the easy way that present-day fabric paints do, and tended to run and blur in the printing, as well as fade with time. Early stencilled pieces were rarely finished off with elaborate trimming or quilting, but tended to be simply hemmed or fringed, although examples have been found where the pattern was worked in as part of a pieced patchwork design.

It is sad that very few early examples of stencilled textiles have survived, but the popularity of the craft was short-lived due to the greater availability of printed textiles. The few that do survive serve as reminders of a very beautiful and exacting craft.

Contemporary Uses and Approaches

Today stencilled textiles are experiencing a revival, largely because of the very effective fabric paints that are widely available. These paints vary in their method of application, their solvency, and their durability, but in general it is now possible to paint and print the most detailed fabric designs and achieve long-lasting results.

The extent of fabric surfaces in the home is nearly equal to the extent of hard surfaces, and the possibilities for stencilling on fabrics are nearly as inexhaustible as the possibilities for stencilling on walls, floors, and furniture. Projects can be small in scale, such as handkerchiefs, ribbons, and pincushions, or they can be on a large scale, such as curtains and bed hangings, but in either case the method of application is the same.

Perhaps the greatest advantage of fabric stencilling is that the size and distribution of a pattern can be altered to fit the proportions of a piece of furniture or a window or a pillow. For example, on a four-poster bed a stencilled pattern can be used to form a neat border on the valences around the top and bottom of the bed. The pattern can then be expanded slightly to decorate the curtains, perhaps more concentrated at the edges and spaced out in the center. The same pattern can then be worked on the bedspread, concentrated on the pillow area or in the center of the bedspread, and used in a border to match the border on the valences. In this way a very balanced and coordinated effect can be achieved which coincides exactly with the dimensions of the bed.

In making pillows and cushions, you can devise a pattern with the exact size of the finished piece in mind, so that the border and interior designs carefully balance. You might use a single border pattern to outline a number of pillows that have been stencilled with different interior motifs to tie them together for a room. Or you could stencil an initial on a pillow and work a decorative pattern around the initial to soften the design. You also could stencil a simple interior motif onto a piece of plain fabric and mount it on a printed fabric that has been used in decorating a room. This would introduce variety to the printed fabric while maintaining a coordinated effect.

The same approach of tailoring a stencil design to specific proportions can be used to make covers for chair seats and footstools in the same way that a piece of embroidery is worked to cover a specific area. Perhaps you have a window seat or a series of window seats that require fitted cushions. Stencilled covers can easily be designed to fit with the dimensions of the area and echo other decorative themes within the room.

One of the most inviting areas to explore in stencilling textiles is outdoor furniture and accessories. Floral and geometric designs lend themselves well to stencilling and can transform the simplest garden furniture. Plain colored canvas suitable for deck chairs and cushions can be cut to size, stencilled, and then applied to furniture, with dynamic results. Designs can range from simple stripes, checks, and polka dots in just one color to elaborate floral and geometric patterns in a wide range of colors. And the same stencil patterns and colors can also be applied to other outdoor equipment—umbrellas, cushions, tables, tablecloths and napkins, dishes, even curtains in a sun room. You might also consider making a floorcloth (see Chapter 6) that picks up the designs of the furniture or curtains.

Fabric stencilling can also be highly attractive on bed linens. The paints used today withstand frequent washing and can be applied to sheets and pillowcases as well as quilts, comforters, and scatter pillows. With time, however, a frequently washed pattern may lose some of its color and look faded next to a less frequently washed item. For this reason, it is a good idea to apply large concentrated areas of pattern to a

Lyn Le Grice designed these coordinating stencils for walls and festoon blinds. The blinds were stencilled with a delicate rose pattern, which was applied around the edges. When the blinds are pulled up, they form a pretty border across the top of the window. *Photo by John Vere Brown.*

quilt or comforter and pick up just one or two elements of the design to use perhaps as a border on a sheet or as a frill on a pillow. Also, because stencilling can leave the fabric slightly stiff where the paint has been applied, it is a good idea not to stencil areas that come in contact with the skin.

An appealing children's comforter could be made to coordinate with the animal border given in the project in Chapter 5. Patterns on quilts and comforters can be split up by using stripes to designate a border in the same way that you can split up a pattern on a floorcloth (see page 109). Or they can be arranged in traditional squares, either printed on the entire piece of fabric or stencilled separately and then joined together, as in a traditional quilt. Old appliqué and Amish quilt patterns provide examples you can imitate with stencilling.

Stencilling can also be applied to a silk or fine cotton or wool fabric to make unique scarves and shawls. You can design a scarf that will coordinate exactly with an outfit you may have. By delicately blending the colors, you can achieve beautiful effects reminiscent of silkscreen printing, at a fraction of the cost of a designer scarf. Buy a little extra fabric so that you can test how the paint will react on the surface. When you have finished the stencilling, you can either fringe or hem the edges of the scarf.

Small household fabric items can be coordinated with other small household items—boxes, canisters, dishes, and so forth. For example, you could use the same stencils featured in the kitchen project in Chapter 4 to coordinate an apron or tea towel as well. Or you could use the rosebud pattern in the same chapter to make a pillow, dressing table mat, or jewelry case coordinate with a bedroom.

So far we have been discussing using stencils on fabric cut to size for a specific purpose and tailoring the pattern to the size of the finished item. Another approach to textile stencilling is to produce lengths of printed fabric or borders that can be cut and used as you would a purchased fabric. When doing this, you should

The same rose pattern was applied to the walls, breaking them up into panels flanking the window. The walls themselves were glazed with a pale straw-colored paint, which softens the delicate stencil pattern even further. *Photo by John Vere Brown.*

keep the pattern simple so that it does not require careful matching and possible wastage, and so that you can print the pattern fast, without meticulous measuring. You can use the stencilled fabric as you would any length of fabric—

A detail of the rose pattern. Lyn Le Grice uses enamel spray paints, which she applies very sparingly through the stencils and which dry almost instantly. Both the walls and the blinds were stencilled with spray paint, and the effect on both surfaces is similar. *Photo by John Vere Brown.*

to make curtains, pillows, bedspreads, and other items.

Stencilling fabrics usually entails some additional sewing to make up the finished piece. Hemming, sewing seams, fringing, piping, quilting, and applying fasteners all might be called for, although it is possible sometimes to stencil onto ready-made but undecorated objects. Fabric can be stencilled either before or after the fabric is assembled and finished, depending on the project in hand. If the finished object can be laid flat, such as a tablecloth, napkin, or unlined curtain, it can be made up first and stencilled afterward. If the stencilled area is part of a more complicated item, such as a frilled or mounted cushion or a quilt, it is best to stencil the piece of fabric (cut to size) first and make up the object afterward.

Details of the motifs used in the center of the panels.

Techniques and Materials

The same principles of design and layout explained in earlier chapters apply equally to tex-

tile stencilling. You will use the same methods of applying borders, turning corners, balancing patterns, deriving pattern ideas, and so forth. However, because textiles present a different type of surface on which to stencil, and fabric paints need some special treatments, textile stencilling requires a slightly different skill.

When you are considering a fabric to stencil, choose one with a flat weave. Stencilling on velvet was and still is a beautiful art, but it requires a different skill because the paint is dabbed onto the surface with a cloth. Generally it is difficult to apply paint to a fabric with a nap. For example, stencilling on towels or a pile rug does not work because the paint merely lies on the surface and easily wears off. The beginner needs to experiment with patterns on flat-weave white cotton until mastering the technique.

Pure fibers are best for stencilling, although you can use cotton mixed with a small proportion of synthetic fiber. (Bear in mind, however, that the fabric paint must be heat sealed, and so the fabric must be able to withstand a hot iron.) Also, the tighter the weave, and hence the more rigid the fabric, the easier it will be to stencil onto. A very pliable fabric will move with the brushstrokes and slip under the stencil. For this reason knitted fabrics are not suitable. Knitted fabrics are also unsuitable because the stencilled pattern lies on the surface of the fabric; when the fabric stretches, the pattern also stretches, allowing unpainted gaps to show.

Any new fabric should be washed before stencilling to remove any surface finish that has been applied and also take care of any potential shrinkage. Once the fabric is washed, you can apply a dye if you want a specific background color. Washing-machine dyes will produce the most even surface color.

To apply the stencil pattern, you should stretch the fabric tight and anchor it. This applies whether you are making a small pillow square or a large bedcover. To do this, you will need a large rectangular pin board or piece of cork—any material that is flat and that pushpins can be stuck into. If you are working with a small piece of fabric, you can anchor it with masking tape around each edge on a drawing board. The purpose of pinning out the piece of fabric is to keep the edges and the grain of the fabric straight so that the stencil design is applied on the straight grain of the fabric. If your piece of fabric is large, you should measure it out into workable units and then align the grain and edge within each unit, which you can then pin, leaving the remainder of the fabric hanging.

Unlike stains on hard surfaces, stains on fabric surfaces cannot readily be removed. When paint is applied, it is there to stay, including mistakes and smudges. It is difficult to remove a paint stain without removing the pattern as well. Keep your hands as free of paint as you can, wiping them frequently, and make sure the backs of your stencils are free of paint. Also, when marking out the surface, never use marker pen; even pencil will be hard to remove. Instead, you need to adopt dressmakers' methods of marking fabric. Notches cut in the seam allowance are good for roughly indicating positioning, and French or tailors' chalk is good for marking points on the surface. The chalk will brush out afterward, but choose the color carefully because dark chalk might leave a mark on a light surface. There are also fabric pencils available in notions shops that can be used for marking. A pressed crease makes a good straight-line indicator, and pins can designate a definite point.

The paint for fabric stencilling is available at most art-supply stores and can also be bought by mail order. Usually it comes in small cans in a variety of colors. Most fabric paints are water soluble in their liquid state, although some of them should be thinned with solvent instead of water; consult the instructions on the can to determine this. Once you have applied the paint, you must fix it into the fibers of the fabric by ironing the painted areas on both sides of the fabric with a warm (350-degree) iron. Again, follow the instructions on the paint container. Like japan colors, fabric paints can be mixed with one another to produce a wide range of colors. While you are stencilling, store mixed colors in small sealed cans or jars and work with smaller quantities poured out on a saucer.

You will be using the same stencil brushes and applying the paint in the same way as in previous projects. You may find, however, that a very wide stencil brush is not satisfactory. The fabric surface creates friction, making the brushwork slightly more difficult, and a large brush might not give you the control you need. As you begin to apply the paint, remember that the fabric will absorb any paint that touches it; if you have a lot of paint in your brush, it will go straight into the fibers and be unevenly distributed. Apply the paint lightly and evenly over the surface at first and then work it in as you like, either shading certain areas or creating a solid effect. Keep your stencilling equipment near you, with paper towels, dishes of paint, brushes, solvent, and teaspoons arranged on a tray.

Sometimes when you are stencilling fabric, the paint will seep through the surface. It is therefore a good idea to slip a sheet of blotting paper under the fabric as you stencil to absorb any excess paint. This is particularly important if you are stencilling one side of a double-thickness piece of fabric. Place several thicknesses of blotting paper between the two layers to prevent the paint from soaking through.

The color of the fabric will affect the colors you use for stencilling. When you are stencilling onto a hard surface, the colors lie on the surface, but in textile stencilling they are absorbed into the fibers. The way in which a stencilled color reacts with a colored ground is discussed in Chapter 2, but in the case of textile stencilling the reaction of the two colors is even more evident. Always test a paint color on a sample of your background fabric, fixing it with a warm iron, to ascertain the outcome before beginning to stencil.

Stencilled fabrics can be washed, either in a washing machine or by hand, using a mild detergent and warm water. Do not wash too vigorously at first, however, until you know how both the fabric and the paint will react. Some brands of paint can also be dry-cleaned. For this and general washing instructions, consult the directions on the paint container.

Tablecloth and napkins designed by Mary MacCarthy for her kitchen table. The pattern on the top of the table consists of a swirling leaf and flower design, and is edged by a harlequin diamond border contained within a double stripe. The same border is repeated around the bottom edge of the tablecloth. Also included in the design are patterned squares of Celtic inspiration, which are printed at intervals within the two borders and in the center of the cloth. The dresser in the background was also stencilled by Mary. *Photo by John Vere Brown.*

project by
Mary MacCarthy

Mary MacCarthy chose for her project a vivid and versatile set of tablecloth and matching napkins. Her pattern was designed especially for her kitchen, to tie in with and enhance the stencilled dresser that already stood in the room and to coordinate with her unusual collection of china.

The project comprises one large circular tablecloth and four napkins. The cloth has one unified design, which was modified for use on the napkins. There is wide flexibility for interpreting the design to fit your needs. By adapting the pattern, you can make the tablecloth rectangular or square, rather than round, and you can make any number of napkins either of the same or different colors of fabric.

The amount of fabric you need will depend on the size of the table you wish the cloth to cover. Mary used 6 yards of 52-inch-wide material for the tablecloth and another 2 yards for the napkins, which are 16-inch squares. The length of the fabric required is determined by its width. First you measure out how many napkins you can fit into the width, and then you can work out how much fabric you will need altogether for cloth and napkins.

For her fabric Mary chose simple pillow ticking—a pure cotton fabric with a tight weave that comes in plain white (the old-fashioned striped ticking is also available but is not really suitable). To achieve exactly the background color she wanted to coordinate with her kitchen, she dyed the ticking with a machine-wash dye. When she found the particular color she wanted for the dye, she realized that it would be too dark if applied full strength, so she diluted the dye more than the recommended strength to achieve a paler result. If you are unsure about dyeing your own fabric, then buy a plain colored cotton fabric in the first place. Because the tablecloth and napkins will be washed frequently, Mary compensated for the inevitable fading by choosing colors for both the dye and the stencilling that are slightly stronger than those she would have used on a hard surface.

Mary derived the ideas for the swirling leaves and flowers in her design from a fifteenth-century screen she saw in a Span-

ish church. She combined this basic pattern with a simple diamond motif for the border to create a more structured overall design. In the center of each napkin and between the double border of the tablecloth, she placed a Celtic square. Rather than mapping out the design inch by inch before applying it, Mary chose to let the pattern evolve itself as she applied it, adapting her original ideas as she went along to fit in the space available. Because you will no doubt be making a tablecloth to fit a specific table, as Mary did, you may likewise want to adapt the pattern to your own dimensions. If you want to make a rectangular or square cloth, you can use the same diamond pattern for the border, but make them and the solid stripes straight rather than curved. The main pattern can still be applied as if to fill a circle in the center, and any gaps at the corners filled with motifs from the pattern if you wish.

If the tablecloth is for a table in your own home, you will be able to do as Mary did and paint the cloth *in situ*. In this way you can maintain a constant picture of how the pattern is turning out, seeing where more pattern is needed and where you have enough. You will notice that Mary's cloth has a border pattern running around the outer edge. To stencil in the border, she brought her ironing board up to the table to extend her work space and moved it around the table as the border progressed. She kept her materials on a cart, close at hand.

When applying a circular border, you must work out how the design will link up at some point. You can do this either by carefully calculating the pattern or by choosing a pattern that is flexible enough to allow for manipulation; a little irregularity can give a pleasing spontaneity to a design. Mary adjusted her pattern as she went along, seeing the effect of the pattern on the table as it evolved. She came up with a double border, an outer one around the hem and an inner one around the edge of the table. The space between the diamonds in the border can then be adjusted if necessary. If you have difficulty making your border designs meet, position the joins of each border so that they are at opposite ends and not doubly conspicuous in the same place.

Mary cut the tablecloth and napkins to size and hemmed them before dyeing or stencilling and therefore she knew the exact space she had available for her pattern. You can easily adapt the pattern and colors to your own needs. If you prefer, you can use fewer colors or omit dyeing the background.

DEGREE OF DIFFICULTY Moderate; successful stencilling on fabric requires some familiarity with stencilling on hard surfaces first, and care needs to be taken to avoid mistakes and smudges.

TIME REQUIRED 4–5 days: washing, dyeing, and drying fabric, 1 day; cutting and stitching fabric, ½ day; ironing, 1 hour; measuring, 1 hour; drawing and cutting stencils, 1 day; assembling materials and work space, 1½ hours; stencilling, 1½–2 days; ironing (fixing), 1 hour

MATERIALS
basic equipment, page 12
4 sheets .0075 acetate or oaktag
6 stencil brushes (¾"–1")
yardstick
tailors' chalk
dressmaking pins
iron
blotting paper
permanent fabric dye (diluted copper)
water or solvent
8 yards cotton ticking (52" wide)

FABRIC PAINTS

light blue	silver gray	rose pink
leaf green	pale yellow	burgundy

1. Preparing the Fabric

Wash your fabric to remove any finish and allow it to dry. Lay the dry fabric flat and iron out the wrinkles. Cut the fabric for the tablecloth according to the size of the table it is to cover or to the given size. Add at least 18 inches extra to all sides of the tabletop to allow for the drop of the cloth and an extra inch more for the hem. (Mary's fabric was cut to a circle 96 inches in diameter.) Then cut out eight squares 17 by 17 inches for the napkins. Hem the tablecloth and each of the napkins.

If you are dyeing the ticking, machine dye the tablecloth and napkins in the same wash to achieve a uniform color. Allow them to dry and press thoroughly to eliminate all creases.

Find the center of the cloth and mark it with a cross, using tailors' chalk. Then mark the position for the inner border; if you are using your table edge as a guide, measure the diameter or width of the table and the diameter or width of the fabric. Subtract the table measurement from the fabric measurement and divide by 2. This will give you the measurement for positioning the inner border. Using a yardstick and tailors' chalk, measure in from the hemmed edge and mark points all around the cloth. Then find and mark the center of each napkin.

2. Making the Stencils

Trace the stencil outlines with pencil onto tracing paper, enlarging them as indicated or as you choose. One large stencil is given here for the pattern in the center of the tablecloth, which is repeated four times. If this seems too large for you to cope with, you can separate it into its various elements and apply them more randomly. Cut a piece of acetate for each stencil, allowing an extra 2 inches all around the design. Trace each outline onto acetate using a drawing pen or permanent marker pen, and label the stencil. You should have six stencils in all.

3. Applying Stencils to the Tablecloth

You will need approximately 4 tablespoons of each paint color—light blue, pale yellow, silver gray, leaf green, rose pink,

Looking down on the tablecloth shows the relationship between the main pattern and the border. Eight Celtic squares occupy the space between the two border patterns, and a ninth one falls in the center. *Photo by John Vere Brown.*

Figure 35 Distribution of patterns on the tablecloth

and burgundy. Assemble your stencilling materials on a tray and transfer small quantities of each color to individual saucers, thinning if necessary. Place the cloth on the table, right side up, and support the edge on an ironing board drawn up to the table. Protect the surface of the ironing board with newspaper.

First apply the outermost border to the tablecloth. Position stencil 1 on the edge of the fabric, anchoring it with masking tape if necessary. Stencil in both solid lines using light blue paint, then move the stencil along the edge of the cloth and continue the lines. Work all the way around the cloth until you reach the starting point and join the lines to make them continuous.

Using the same stencil, apply the diamonds between the lines, using different or alternating colors for each of the diamonds. Work around the edge in the same way and adjust the spacing if necessary as you reach your starting point. Use a clean brush for each color, and take care not to smudge one color into the next opening in the stencil. If necessary, mask out adjacent openings with a scrap of stencil material.

Following your chalk markings for the inner border, apply the inner diamond border (stencil 2) in the same way. Use the same blue, or a different color if you prefer, for the solid lines and alternate colors for the diamonds.

Next position the Celtic square (stencil 3) in the center of the cloth. Apply the outer solid border in light blue paint, pulling the stencil across at each corner and painting in the bridge area so that the lines meet. Then stencil in the inner pattern using green and yellow paint, being careful not to smudge paint into adjacent openings. If you prefer, you can separate this pattern into two stencils. The same Celtic square is then applied at eight points around the cloth, between the two borders. Mark eight evenly spaced points in the "drop" area of the cloth with tailors' chalk. Then apply the stencil, turning it so that it prints as a diamond and varying the colors as you wish. Using a contrasting color, apply the dot stencil (stencil 4) in the center of each of the nine Celtic squares.

To apply the main stencil (stencil 5) to the middle of the cloth, you may have to juggle with the stencil to establish the position in which it should be printed. Mary achieved four repeats within her inner border. If your cloth is larger, you may want to extend the pattern by repeating a few additional elements of the design. If it is smaller, you may want to omit some of the elements. Mark the four positions roughly with tailors' chalk. Then start to stencil in the pattern. Use different colors for the flowers and light green for the leaves, masking

Colors for the pattern were chosen so that they balance in the overall design. While green was used for the stems throughout, pink, rust, yellow, and dark and light blue were used for the flowers and leaves. The same colors were repeated in the harlequin border. *Photo by John Vere Brown.*

any areas where you think you might smudge. If you find you have gaps where the stencils join up, fill them with extra leaf or flower prints. Using the small flower center (stencil 6), apply contrasting colors for the centers of the flowers. The stencilling on the cloth is now complete.

4. Applying Stencils to the Napkins

Lay one napkin on a flat surface that has been protected with newspaper. Position the Celtic square (stencil 3) over the middle of the napkin and apply the center part of the pattern (not the stripe border) in the same way as before, using the colors you prefer. Then apply the central dot (stencil 4). If desired, enlarge the square to create a border stripe around the edge. Position the corner stencil (stencil 7) around one corner and stencil in the pattern, using one or more colors as you choose. Then position the stencil around the opposite corner and apply it in the same way, using either the same or different colors. Apply the dot (stencil 4) to the middles of the flowers and two corners. Stencil the remaining three napkins, using either the same color combinations or a different one for each napkin.

Each of the four napkins uses a different color interpretation of the design. The stripe border around the edge was taken from the Celtic square pattern, which was separated and the center part placed in the center of the napkin. *Photo by John Vere Brown.*

5. Fixing the Paint

Iron the tablecloth on the wrong side first, holding the iron over the painted areas for a few seconds to bond the paint into the fibers. Turn the cloth and repeat on the other side. Iron the napkins in the same way.

Stencil 5

The stencils that Mary MacCarthy used for her tablecloth and napkins. *Photo by John Vere Brown.*

Stencils and designs © 1987 by Mary MacCarthy

Stencil 1

Stencil 2

Enlarge stencil 3 350% for "drop" area, and 250% for tablecloth center and napkins. Enlarge all other stencils 250%.

Stencil 3

Stencil 4

Stencil 6

Stencil 7

155

Motifs from the stencilled borders in this room have been arranged to make an area of concentrated pattern over the mirror. *Photo © Elizabeth Whiting & Associates.*

Opposite page: Mary MacCarthy applied a stencilled motif uniformly over the walls and a different border pattern around the windows of the landing in her cottage. The stencilled motif compensates for the unevenness of the old walls. *Photo by John Vere Brown.*

CHAPTER NINE
Walls

"Whatever you have in your rooms, think first of the walls, for they are that which makes your house a home." So advised William Morris, dean of the Arts and Crafts movement in late-nineteenth-century Britain. Perhaps more than any other surface, walls offer the greatest scope to the stencil artist.

It was primarily walls that received the first strokes of the stencilling brush. In Europe the art goes back to medieval times, when stencilling was used as a means of decorating churches and other religious buildings.

In America, wall stencilling dates back to the early eighteenth century, when colonists were seeking a rudimentary way of bringing color and decoration into their houses. Before then their resources had permitted little in the way of adornment, but as news spread of the growing fashion for lavish wallpapers and wall decor in Europe, the early Americans longed for a touch of ornament in their otherwise sparse homes. A market developed for itinerant stencillers who would travel the countryside seeking board and lodging in return for their skill with the stencil brush. Although patterns at this time imitated the designs and forms prevalent in Europe, their means of execution, by necessity, gave them a simple and unsophisticated character.

Many of the techniques we practice today we owe to the skill of those early craftsmen. Through their clear and honest designs—the majority based on the natural forms around them—we can see the basic steps involved in devising a stencil pattern, one which, despite its repetitive method of application, possesses great movement and has impact.

In stencilling a wall, more than any other surface, you must be aware of the differing impacts of pattern formations and the effects of presenting the same pattern in a variety of ways. When itinerant stencillers called on houses, they presented their clients with an array of stencils that in effect represented their trademark. From this array clients could choose a particular theme or collection of outlines that complemented or repeated existing patterns or themes within their homes.

Stencilled walls can be as lavish or as subtle as you choose. The tremendous variety of patterns means that whether you are decorating a

157

period drawing room or a children's playroom, the effect can always be original. The beauty of stencilling walls lies in the fact that the pattern is tailor-made for the room. Structural flaws and inconsistencies can be overcome much more easily when a wall is stencilled than when it is papered. In some old houses you cannot use certain patterns of wallpaper because of the angle of the corners or the slope of the floor, and it is better to have a plain wall that will not emphasize the imperfections. Wall stencilling provides a wonderful means of introducing pattern into such a room.

Developing a Pattern

Choosing a pattern for stencilling your walls is a matter of narrowing down the multitude of possibilities open to you. First, as when choosing a wallpaper, you must decide what effect you would like in a room. Do you want it to be bold or flamboyant, sporadic or allover, seasonal or topical, naive or sophisticated, colorful or subdued, and so forth. You would ask yourself these questions when choosing a fabric or wallpaper also, but for a stencilling project your answers are the beginning to your design.

Then you must look around your room and decide whether you want existing colors to determine the color scheme you choose, and if so, which ones. You might decide that your stencil design is to be the focus of the room and that everything else will have to coordinate with it. Or you may already have a carpet that is to be the determining factor in your choice of color. Perhaps your curtains, or even something as small as a pillow ornament, will act as your color guide. Again, this decision is bringing you one step closer to working out your own design.

Once you have decided on the color and effect that are best for your room, you can set about choosing a pattern for stencilling. Many precut stencils translate well into overall wall stencils if you use collections of motifs in a planned sequence. For example, you might want to stencil a bouquet or wreath of flowers on one

or more walls in a room—perhaps at the end of a hallway or down each side of a corridor. You could arrange a group of smaller individual precut stencils into either the wreath or bouquet shape yourself, just as you would a bunch of flowers. With the arrangement mapped out, you can then repeat it as planned on the walls to give an original effect. Similarly, you could take the same stencils and arrange them in a swag or garland to be applied just below the ceiling, all around a room. Or you could bring the collection of flowers down in vertical stripes at intervals across a wall surface.

In early American times, wall stencilling usually duplicated a wallpaper effect by repeating a given design or sequence of designs in an arrangement of vertical lines around a room. Today, with sophisticated wallpaper production and a wide range of wallpaper patterns available, people choose stencilling for an effect that is different from, rather than imitative of, wallpaper. Wall stencilling is not limited to the mechanical repetition of a motif, but instead offers the possibility of combining a series of elements imaginatively within the boundary of the wall.

Stencilling a wall can be much more like painting a picture, because it allows you to compose an overall effect that would not be possible with wallpaper. You can have a border running around the ceiling, and perhaps a thematically related border at chair-rail height or at the baseboard. Then to fill the area between chair rail and ceiling, you can introduce a larger single element, repeated along the wall at intervals. Or if you want more of an art nouveau effect, you can start your pattern at the baseboard and allow it to grow randomly upward in waves, tapering away up the wall. If you were stencilling a wall in a children's room, you could take a variety of motifs and arrange them in a typical setting, such as a farmyard or house, so that the whole wall would become a picture.

It is important when designing a wall stencil to balance the proportions of the design with the proportions of the wall. If you are designing your own pattern, constantly pin a sketch of the pro-

Clear, bright colors have been used in this contemporary rendering of a traditional wall stencil by Virginia Teichner. Individual elements have been arranged in vertical lines, with vertical and horizontal stencilled borders separating the overall pattern. *Photo by David Arky.*

A lattice stencil with intertwining flowers and tendrils covers a kitchen wall in the 1985 Kipps Bay Show House. *Photo by Dennis Krukowski.*

A detail of the lattice design. *Photo by Dennis Krukowski.*

posed outline to the wall to ensure that its size corresponds to the scale of the wall. A design can become lost on a large expanse.

Preparing the Wall Surface

Walls that will be stencilled should have a matte finish and can be painted with a flat oil-based or latex paint. You can also stencil onto paneled wood walls using the same approach as for wooden floors. If you choose to leave the wood unpainted, you should sand it well and wipe with a tack cloth. If a stain is required, apply it before stencilling. A coat of varnish should be brushed over the wooden surface when the stencilling is complete. Wooden surfaces can also be painted, in which case the rules of matte finish apply. Stencilling does not require varnishing if the wall has been painted.

Applying stencils to a rough stone or very coarsely plastered wall is not always easy, but a very soft effect can be achieved with spray paint, which sits on the surface and does not require constant daubing with a stencil brush. A wall painted with sand paint can also look very effective when stencilled because the stencilling takes on a slightly fuzzy look. Glossy wall surfaces are not suitable because the paint does not adhere and drips under the stencil openings.

Planning the Distribution of Stencils

As when marking out a stencilled floor, you need to enlist help when planning your design on a wall. It is necessary to use a plumb line to achieve accurate vertical measurements and markings, and although you can do this single-handedly, the job is much easier and more successful with another person's help.

Although it is important to have your stencilled design balanced and in proportion, you need not go to great extremes to measure down to the last half inch. Always bear in mind that the charm of stencilling lies in its handcrafted effect. Had you wanted total perfection, you probably would have bought an elaborate wallpaper and hired a professional to apply it. The effect of stencilling should be artistic and personal, and not that of a manufactured product. Therefore, when doing your initial measuring, you need to assess the dimensions of your room and the walls and then determine if there are features in the room that will influence the positioning of your design.

Centering your design, as always, is the key to balancing it, but this does not mean that you must find the exact center. In the project that begins on page 163, when Kate Williams evaluated the wall to be stencilled, she realized that the light fixture over the table was not exactly in the center of the wall and yet it was important that the light shine directly over the table. Since the light fixture pulled the eye away from the direct center, she compromised in marking the center of the wall so that the pattern and light coincided. (For our photograph, the light was lifted away from the wall to reveal the pattern.)

Once you have measured the height and length of the wall and estimated the center, you are ready to fit your stencilling to the wall. Mark horizontal lines with a ruler or yardstick and vertical lines with a plumb line. If your pattern includes a border at ceiling height, you should center the border first and adjust the pattern so that it fits comfortably. If there is no border, measure out to either side of the center, using a ruler or tape measure, and mark the wall lightly with pencil or chalk. Once the border is established (even if not yet stencilled), you can use it as your guide for any vertical stencils you intend to use.

Use a plumb line to mark the vertical lines, following the instructions on page 25. It is important that you hold the plumb line taut once you have allowed it to drop and hang still. Both the person at the top and the person at the bottom should hold it against the wall. Snap it cleanly and swiftly to achieve a well-defined line, then move on to the next line to be marked.

Once you have established the distribution of the vertical lines, you can consider the positioning of your pattern on the wall. It is a good idea to stagger the positions of the stencils, because a motif repeated at the same height all around can become monotonous. This is demonstrated in the project that follows where the main element of the design, a medallion of leaves and flowers, alternates in position across the wall, higher in one place, lower in the next.

If your pattern is more like the early American stencils and is to be arranged in vertical lines descending from the border, then you simply work down the vertical chalk lines, making sure that the positioning of each element corresponds with similar elements in the previous line. If your wall stencil is to include a border just above the baseboard, you should apply this after you have finished the vertical lines. Again, use the center vertical line as your centering device and work out evenly to either side of this point.

Dealing with Corners

When stencilling a pattern onto a wall, you may encounter problems as you reach a corner. If your pattern does not end either just before or right on the corner, you will have to decide how to overcome this predicament. Your decision will depend largely on the architecture of your room. If the corner is just a straightforward corner where two main walls meet, you can bend the stencil and work evenly to either side so that the pattern moves from one wall to the next. If, however, your corner is caused by an architectural element such as a jutting-out arch, then it makes sense to stop at the corner, bending and masking out the remainder of the stencil. You can, if you wish and if the wall permits, continue the remainder of the stencil on the wall to the other side of the arch, as was done in the following project. If when you reach your corner you are faced with a window or door frame, then you are forced to print only half the stencil, again blocking out the part that would go around the corner.

In Kate Williams's design for stencilled dining room walls, the dentil and swag borders repeat across the top at fixed intervals, while the remaining motifs alternate to add movement and interest to the design. *Photo by David Arky.*

project by
Kate Williams

Kate Williams's design for stencilled walls combines both architectural motifs and stylized swags and vines, resulting in a feeling that is both classical and contemporary. The combination of geometric and natural forms is an interesting one and lends itself to a range of interpretations. As executed here, it creates an atmosphere of poise and freshness in an apartment room that might otherwise seem plain and dark.

Kate used the dentil ornament around the tops of the walls to introduce architectural details into her apartment, which had little in the way of structural ornamentation. The rooms are sufficiently high to respond well to this type of *trompe l'oeil* treatment, which, when seen from a distance, gives a very realistic impression of a carved dentil cornice. This dentil border can be used in a *trompe l'oeil* sense in any room, with or without the addition of any further decorative patterns. It adds a feeling of grandeur and historic detail and would be particularly suitable for a hallway or staircase. *Trompe l'oeil* treatments work best when viewed from a distance, and care has to be taken to make sure that the proportions of the room are adequate. This dentil would not work in an intimate, low-ceilinged room.

The method of cutting and executing the dentil border is one of the simplest techniques in this book, and yet the effect can be highly realistic. You can easily reduce or enlarge the pattern, which requires little in the way of centering and measuring. To achieve the effect of plaster or stone moldings, the design should be executed in pale shades of gray, beige, pink, or blue, depending on the background color of the walls. Each dentil here is made up of three stencilled areas, each a different shade of bluish-white, to create the effects of light and shadow in a three-dimensional form. However, if you wish to diverge from this mock architectural effect, you can turn the design into a lively three-dimensional geometric border by using a contrasting color in each of the three stencils.

The vine swag is an elementary stencil that similarly can be used in a variety of ways. It is simple to cut and simple to execute. Used here, it sets the pace for the distribution of the remaining pattern on the wall. A swag is useful in any stencil design, and its curving form introduces a feeling of rhythm and movement that is often lacking in the repetitive application of stencil motifs. Separating each swag is a simple ball, painted in a lively blue to add some depth of color and subtly shaded to give a three-dimensional, sphere-like effect.

The focus of Kate's design is the decorative garland medallion placed at intervals across the wall. This motif requires a slightly more complex stencilling technique, both in cutting and execution, but it provides an opportunity to see the way in which a very painterly effect can be achieved with stencils alone. The nucleus of the design is a delicate lyre inspired by a similar form in the silver candlesticks on the table. This shows how you can find design ideas in your home that are of particular sentimental value or are particularly pleasing and versatile. After translating the lyre into a stencil outline, Kate surrounded it with a flourish of color in the form of a garland of leaves and flowers, thus making the motif more substantial and conspicuous.

The final motif in this design is a small crimson emblem— a simple outline that introduces a lively contrast of color and prevents the design from becoming too monotone. You can choose almost any outline you like, but this one is particularly successful in providing depth for the design through its vertical emphasis. It is placed to lead the eye downward, counteracting the upward sweep of the swag.

One of the distinguishing features of Kate Williams's stencilling technique is her delicate blending of the pastel colors she frequently uses. If you examine the main garland medallion carefully, you will see that the flowers and buds of the design are a subtle blend of pink and blue and white. Kate achieves this by working from a palette of colors rather than individual pots of different paints for specific areas. In this way the colors are constantly mixed and tinted as she applies them.

Kate will also frequently use two brushes to paint within one stencil outline—one for each of two colors, which are blended within the stencil opening. This is not a difficult technique to master and introduces a variety of ways of diverging from your original design.

DEGREE OF DIFFICULTY Moderate

TIME REQUIRED 3½–6 days: measuring and marking wall, ½–1 day; making stencils, 1 day; applying stencils, 2–4 days, depending on room size

MATERIALS
basic equipment, page 12
2 sheets .0075 acetate
plumb line and chalk box
5 stencil brushes (½"–1½")
stepladder
turpentine or paint thinner
leftover background paint

JAPAN COLORS

white	CP green dark
ultramarine blue	raw umber
lamp black	cadmium yellow medium
poster red	

ARTISTS' OILS
alizarin crimson
permanent violet

Note: For tinting, you can substitute artists' oil paint for any of the above colors with the exception of white and black, but remember that if you want a particularly deep color, the oil paint will slow down the drying properties of the japan color considerably. These are suggested colors that have been mixed to produce the colors in this project. You may vary them as you choose.

1. Making the Stencils

Trace and enlarge each of the stencil outlines as indicated or to the size you require.

Cut pieces of acetate for each of the stencils, allowing at least a 2-inch border all around the design. Trace each stencil outline onto a piece of acetate, labeling each and including any relevant registration marks.

Cut out each stencil using a utility knife.

2. Preparing the Surface

In this case the surface was freshly painted with light bluish-violet flat oil-based paint. Whatever your choice, make sure the surface is clean and dry. A gloss or even semi-gloss surface will not accept wall stencilling successfully.

3. Marking the Surface for the Border

Depending on the size of the dentil stencil you decide on for your room, measure approximately 1 inch and 3 inches down from the ceiling all around the walls, using a ruler and

Taking the borders around a corner, matching the patterns on each side.
Photo by David Arky.

yardstick. Mark the intermittent points on the walls every 9 inches or so. Measure the length of each wall, and on paper work out the number of dentils and spaces you will be able to fit into each stretch of wall. Mark the starting point.

4. Applying the Dentil Border

You will need three shades of one color for the dentil border. In this instance, Kate used three shades of pale bluish-white. The main square is the lightest shade, which in this case is virtually white; the side shadow is the medium shade; and the bottom shadow is the darkest. To mix your colors on the palette, start with three separate dollops of white japan paint and tint each with tiny quantities of ultramarine blue and either lamp black or raw umber until you have the desired three shades of color.

First apply the main square (stencil 1) across the top of each wall using the lightest shade of paint. Then, using these squares for registration, apply the medium shade to the side stencil and then the darkest shade to the bottom stencil.

5. Marking Out the Rest of the Wall

You can now use the row of dentils to measure the positions of the remaining stencils. To balance the design, start at the center of the wall and work outward. Using Kate's proportions, the curved swag falls every five dentils. Three swags (and hence fifteen dentils) make up one unit of her design, which also includes one entire medallion and six crimson motifs. With the dentils stencilled in position, you are ready to mark the vertical sections of the wall with the chalk box.

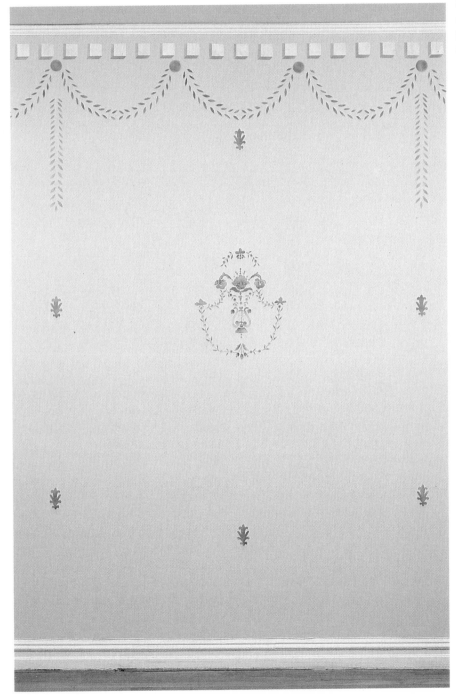

One complete element of the design showing how the pattern is distributed from the dentils downward. *Photo by David Arky.*

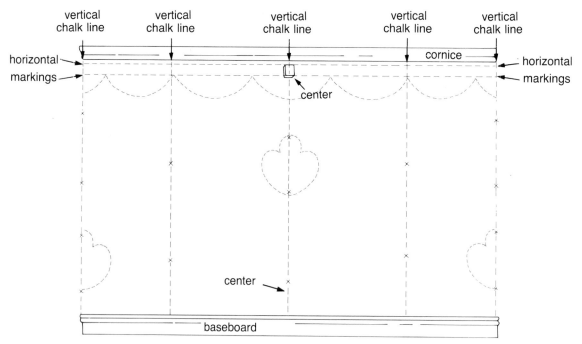

vertical chalk line   vertical chalk line   vertical chalk line   vertical chalk line   vertical chalk line

horizontal markings

cornice

horizontal markings

center

center

baseboard

Figure 36 Marking out the wall

Within one unit of fifteen dentils the pattern subdivides into three areas of five dentils. Each swag spans virtually five dentils and has a blue ball between the fifth and the sixth. You will need to use a plumb line and chalk box to mark vertical lines at the beginning and end of the fifteen dentils and a third vertical in the center of these two. Refer to figure 36 for the exact positioning of your vertical chalk lines. Repeat this pattern across the wall as necessary, working out to either side of the center.

6. Completing the Stencilling

With the vertical lines mapped out on the wall, you can complete the stencilling. Mix dark green paint for the leaves of the vine swag using CP green dark, lamp black, and a tiny amount of ultramarine and burnt umber. Follow the instructions in Chapter 2 for mixing colors and experiment on paper before applying them to the wall. Stencil in the vine swags (stencil 4) as indicated, leaving room for the blue balls. Then stencil in the vertical vines (stencil 5) at the first and every following fifteenth dentil using the same shade of green. Using a bright and quite strong mix of ultramarine blue and white, stencil in the balls (stencil 6) between the swags, shading the paint within the stencil to create a three-dimensional effect.

On the center vertical chalk line, mark the height at which you would like the garland medallion to fall. Kate chose to stagger the positioning of these medallions so that in one place they were positioned approximately three feet above the baseboard, and at the next approximately one foot above the baseboard. This gives some movement to the design. Three stencils are involved in the printing of the medallion—one for the leaves, stems, and lyre; one for the berries; and one for the flowers.

First apply the outer leaf boundary (stencil 7). Center this on the chalk line and fix it firmly to the wall with masking tape. The leaves are painted in the same dark green as the swags. Use a darker green or dull brown for the stems of the leaves. Use small stencil brushes and take care not to smudge into adjacent stencil openings. Then apply the berries (stencil 8) using the same bright blue that you used for the balls. Follow the close-up photograph to see the colors in each section of the stencil, and where two are blended, use a separate brush for each color. Next, apply the pink flowers and buds (stencil 9), using a rose pink color and blending it with touches of mauve, paler pink, and light blue. Then apply the outer bows of the lyre (stencil 7 again) in a pale pink base, tinted with touches of blue. Finally, stencil in the harp strings in deeper blue.

Detail of the garland medallion showing how the paint is blended and shaded within the flowers and how the lyre comes together. *Photo by David Arky.*

Elaborating the basic design with freehand painting. *Photo by David Arky.*

There is much scope for hand painting when applying this stencil, and those who feel capable will be able to elaborate on the design at each stage, as well as improvise with colors. Freehand painting can also eliminate some of the more intricate stencil cutting and thereby speed up this stage.

Finally, mark the positions for the deep pink emblems (stencil 10) on the vertical chalk lines. The exact placement is a matter of choice; Kate has them positioned above and below the garland medallion and with two more to either side. It is important that they are level as they repeat along the wall, but they can alternate in height to introduce movement.

7. Finishing Off

Wall stencilling does not require a finish. The project is complete when dry.

Caring for the walls Stencilled walls can be washed after about four to six months if necessary. Do not use detergent, which will damage the painted surface. A mild soap and water solution applied with a soft sponge is best.

Stencil 4

Sample print

Enlarge all stencils 155%

Sample print

Stencil 5

Stencils and designs © 1987 by Kate Williams

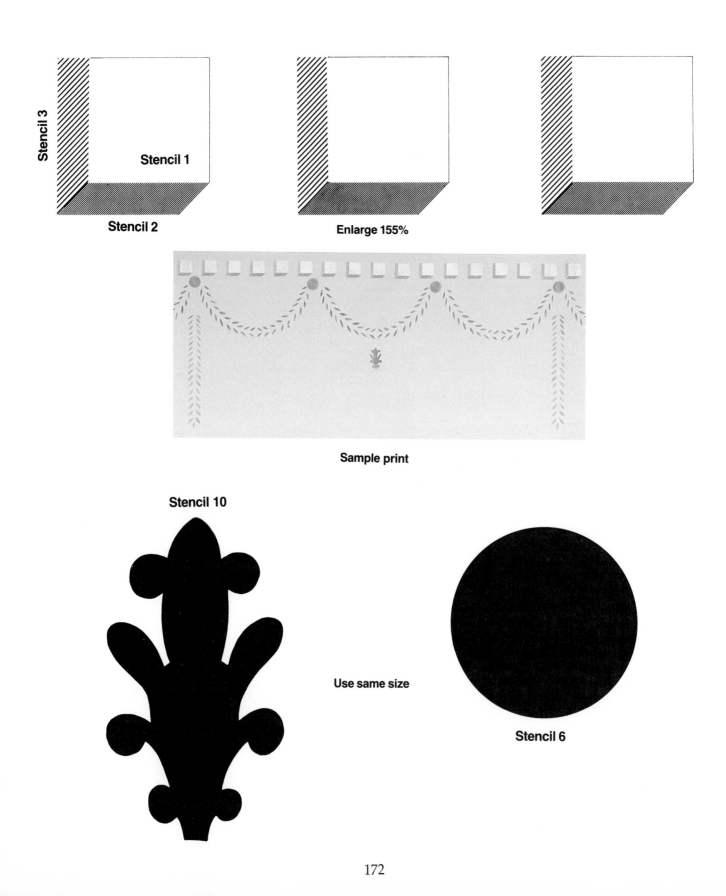

Stencil 3

Stencil 1

Stencil 2

Enlarge 155%

Sample print

Stencil 10

Use same size

Stencil 6

172

Enlarge 155%

Stencil 7

Stencil 8

Stencil 9

Cile Lord designed this extraordinary floor stencil for a model room in Bloomingdale's.
Photo courtesy Cile Lord.

Opposite page: Detail of a Chinese-influenced motif stencilled on a stained wood floor by
Cile Lord. *Photo by Edward Hardin.*

CHAPTER TEN
Floors

Some of the earliest examples of stencilling appear on floors, as well as on walls. In colonial America, when carpets were scarce and unaffordable and wood was plentiful, people decorated their wooden floors with paint. The unchangeably hard surface of the wood lent itself to primitive imitations of carpet patterns, which were applied as borders along the outside of the floor or as simple tile-like patterns over the entire surface. Early floor stencil patterns were frequently simple and geometric—perhaps a central pattern of diamonds in alternating colors inspired by black-and-white tile patterns and enclosed by a geometric border. Some historic examples of lavish floors entailing layers and layers of elaborate stencilling would prove a challenge to even the most proficient stenciller today.

Today stencilled floors offer a multitude of design possibilities—some complex and detailed, others economical but highly effective for decorating a bare expanse of floor. Wooden floors are again in vogue, and modern sanding techniques can restore an old floor previously covered by layers of adhesive and linoleum and make it look sparkling new. Stencilling can be an in-

centive for delving beneath the layers and rejuvenating a room from the floor up.

There are a variety of approaches to stencilling a floor and decorating a room to coordinate with it. One approach is to stencil the floor in a detailed and colorful pattern that becomes the focus of the room and to tie all other decorations in with it. Another approach is to choose a combination of papers and fabrics for the walls and furnishings and to place an equal strength of pattern on the floor so that the entire room coordinates. A third approach is to create a strong impact with your walls or fabrics, keeping the remainder of the furnishings plain, and add a delicate pattern to the floor that just complements the other decorations. A final approach is to have an overall minimalist effect with stark walls and just the subtlest hint of pattern stencilled on the floor, perhaps in two similar shades applied for a transparent effect.

Whatever your choice, stencilling a floor is always an economical means of finishing off a room. The only drawback is that it is not transportable. But if you do hit upon a design that ties in with your other furnishings, you should take good care of your stencils. Then if you move, you can duplicate the design on the new floor, which will once again coordinate with your decor.

Stencilling a floor is also an ideal way to add color to rooms that get a lot of wear and tear and yet deserve to be decorated. Children's rooms, playrooms, bathrooms, kitchens, and back hallways all look better with stencilled floors, which can tolerate frequent cleaning. The polyurethane used to seal the floor makes the wood resistant to water. This is not to say, however, that a stencilled floor will withstand a thorough soaking. In a bathroom it is advisable to keep mats scattered over the floor to absorb sporadic deluges.

Lynn Goodpasture stencilled this pattern on a floor to fill the space between the carpet and the wall. *Photo by David Arky.*

Another approach to stencilling a wooden floor is simply to stencil a border around the outside. In a dining room, for example, where much of the center of the floor is obscured by a table, it is sufficient and very effective to stencil only around the perimeter. Similarly, if you have a square or rectangle of plain colored carpet that does not reach to the walls, you can stencil a pattern on the floor to fill the space between the carpet and the walls. This is an ingenious way of picking up a design in a curtain or bedspread fabric when the walls and carpet are plain. It serves to tie in a theme without overwhelming the room.

Floor stencils can be colorful and dominating or subtle and enhancing. You can choose colors that are vibrant and playful, covering the entire floor surface, or you can use the stencil to stain only selected areas, leaving the natural color of the floor to show through in places. You can apply the paint opaquely so that the grain of the wood is completely obscured, or you can apply it thinly so that the grain remains visible.

Today there are a great many paints and stains available that are suitable for floor painting. Most of them are oil-based, and for stencilling a design, you should use japan color whenever possible because of its quick-drying properties. Although you are covering a large area when stencilling a floor, the drying properties of the paint remain important simply because you often find yourself having to kneel or tread on areas that have just been stencilled.

Preparing a Wood Floor

Unfortunately, it is not possible simply to stencil onto an existing floor surface unless it is completely new and unfinished. Ingrained wax, grease, and dirt repel paint when it is applied, and more often than not, a stencil will not last. Moreover, it is preferable to stencil onto as smooth a surface as possible. Splinters and indentations not only will result in an uneven print, but also will play havoc with your brushes. It is therefore advisable to have a floor freshly sanded before embarking on your stencilling project. Although you can do this chore yourself with a sanding machine, it is a difficult task that creates quantities of dust, and you might prefer having it done professionally. Make sure that the floor is not sanded with too fine a sandpaper, which will leave a silky finish on the wood and make stencilling difficult, as a glossy surface does. Vacuum the floor thoroughly when the sanding is complete and wipe it with a tack cloth before applying any paint.

After the floor is sanded, you can choose from a variety of ways to finish the wooden surface before stencilling. One treatment, among the most popular in the past, is to paint the entire floor to provide a background color for the stencilling. Usually a flat oil-based paint is used, and the floor may require two coats to make an even base. Oil-based paint takes a while to dry, though, and so to speed up the process you can use latex paint, but the surface will be less durable, partly because of the nature of the paint and partly because the water in the paint raises the grain of the wood somewhat. You should lightly sand the painted surface after it has dried in areas where the grain is raised. The floor in Virginia Teichner's border project in Chapter 5 was treated with oil-based paint.

The trend today is toward retaining at least some of the natural grain of the wood, so that the stencilling gently floats over the wooden surface. This gives a much lighter effect and can be achieved in a number of ways.

BLEACHING Bleaching provides a natural means of lightening the color of a freshly sanded floor. Oak takes most successfully to bleaching and results in a cream color. Pine tends to take on a yellowish tinge. It is better that you have bleaching done professionally because it entails the use of caustic materials that should not be inhaled. Sand the floor lightly when the bleaching is complete.

SIMULATED BLEACHING This method of delicately staining a floor has the effect of bleaching but requires no professional treatment. A thin coat of pale-cream flat oil-based paint is wiped

This stencilled floor design executed by Cile Lord gives the effect of a stained pattern on the wooden surface. *Photo by David Arky.*

off with a rag almost as soon as you apply it, while the paint is still very wet. It is important to keep the paint uniform as you progress from one area to the next and have a good supply of rags on hand for wiping. If the floor is not as pale as you would like, you can repeat the process. This is quite time-consuming and tiring work, so restrict it to smaller floors or enlist help.

Lynn Goodpasture stencilled the floor of her bathroom with a bamboo-like crisscross design interrupted with a delicately colored and shaded shell form. The wooden surface of the floor was bleached first and then stained with white before the stencils were applied, then the entire surface was varnished. *Photo by David Arky.*

A detail of the shell pattern. *Photo by David Arky.*

STAINING The wide range of colored stains on the market today can be used either to introduce color into a wooden floor or to simulate a certain type of wood. Available at most hardware stores, these oil-based stains are readily absorbed into the newly sanded surface of the wood. They do not affect any paint subsequently stencilled onto the floor.

Always buy a test can of stain first, because the color swatches displayed with the stains do not always accurately indicate how a particular stain will react on your floor. Apply stain evenly to the floor with a wide, flat paintbrush and allow it to dry thoroughly before attempting to stencil. Follow the advice on the can for the quantity of stain required for your floor area. Always apply stain with the grain of the wood, never across it.

GLAZING Glazing is a method of applying color to a floor that creates a translucent effect. First the newly sanded floor is given an opaque coat of white or pale cream flat oil-based paint. A thin wash-like mixture of colored paint is then applied over the dry opaque surface, which gives depth to the color. The wash is made by tinting oil sealer with a small quantity of japan paint or a mixture of japan paint and artists' oils. Glazing can also be used on furniture (see Lynn Goodpasture's project in Chapter 7).

Labor-Saving Hints

Stencilling a floor is quite a strenuous project, and whenever possible you should enlist help from someone else, at least to get started. Measuring and marking a floor is done with the aid of a plumb line and chalk box, as explained on page 25. If you are stencilling a floor for the first time, you will definitely need help with marking the floor and possibly with the actual stencilling. Even when you are more practiced, you will need someone to hold the other end of the plumb line and snap it.

Stencilling a floor also entails a certain amount of acrobatics. You must step around wet stencils and bend and kneel a lot while working. In the project that follows, Cile Lord recommends that you wear a clean pair of inexpensive white cotton socks so that the wet stencils are not smudged or damaged if you tread on them. The socks will also keep your feet clean and prevent dust particles from spreading into the wet paint. Another helpful hint of hers is to wear a pair of knee pads while stencilling so that you don't have to keep picking up and putting down a kneeling pad that might smudge your work. Knees tend to suffer when you are stencilling an entire floor.

Finishing and Maintaining a Floor

When a floor has been stencilled, it must be sealed with varnish to protect the stencilled pattern and the wood surface. The majority of varnishes have a polyurethane base of some sort, and they are available in matte, semi-gloss, and gloss finishes. For most stencilling projects a semi-gloss effect is ideal; the floor surface looks clean and polished but not glassy.

Buy a good-quality varnish that is clear, with as little yellow tint as possible. Varnish always casts a yellowish hue, which will affect the colors underneath. Bear this in mind when first choosing your colors, and experiment with both paint and varnish before stencilling so that you know what results will look like.

Allow the stencilling to dry at least twenty-four hours, longer in humid weather. Using a wide, flat paintbrush, apply the varnish evenly, working with the grain of the wood. Test a small area over the stencilling first to make sure that no bleeding occurs. (See page 31 for solutions to bleeding problems.) Always follow the instructions on the can for application, drying times, and quantities. For speed, you can apply varnish with a roller, but the effect will not be as smooth. A floor needs at least two coats of varnish. Never apply the second coat until the first one is quite dry.

A polyurethaned floor can be sponge-mopped with a weak solution of soap or detergent and water, but avoid drenching it. Do not use wax or wax-based floor-cleaning solutions because the layer of wax will resist any future touch-ups of varnish or paint. If your floor dulls considerably with wear, you can apply a new coat of the same varnish to restore its gleam.

From time to time check the varnished surface for signs of wear, and revarnish before the stencilling is exposed. Store samples of the background and stencilling paints, or make notations of the mixtures so you can patch a floor that gets badly scratched.

Design for a kitchen floor by Cile Lord. The floor was first stained and then the crisscross stencil design applied over it in off-white. The double-stripe border was applied in a thin coat of raw umber paint so that the grain of the wood would show through. The pattern was reduced to fill the smaller area of floor near the doorway. *Photo by David Arky.*

project by Cile Lord

Although this design by Cile Lord is straightforward, it can be used in a variety of ways. As executed here, it was an effective way to decorate an otherwise plain stained-wood kitchen floor. The owner wanted to retain the natural feeling of the wooden cabinets and floor as well as the simplicity of the plain white walls, while introducing an element of pattern to liven up the kitchen. Because the floor, a mixture of pine and oak, was old, it was professionally sanded and then stained (in a medium walnut) to give uniformity to the two different types of wood.

Cile's design lends itself to a range of color interpretations. In this instance she used a cream-colored paint for the main stencil pattern, subtly accenting it with a central dot of burnt umber. The surrounding border stripe was painted in the same burnt umber, and the corner ball in the border picked up the cream of the main stencil. While the stencil is lighter, the border is darker than the floor stain, and the three colors balance well without any of them seeming lost.

The beauty of this design, however, is that it can be executed in stronger, more vibrant colors without making the floor seem overpowering. The design would work well in deep shades of red, green, and blue, for example. The background color of the floor could be deep red, with the crisscrosses and corner balls in green and the borders and dots in blue. Or you could use just two colors—perhaps a white background with the pattern in indigo—for a clean, summery effect.

Remember, too, that this is a pattern that would work well on other surfaces. It is easy to scale down and can be used without the border. It would be an ideal pattern to stencil onto fabric. Consider painting the floor of a room with both pattern and border and then using the main pattern alone on plain curtains with a similar background color. The same design would make a beautiful tablecloth and napkins—or even sheets. A shower curtain could be stencilled to coordinate with a bathroom floor.

It is a basic design that lends itself to scaling up and scaling down and to a wide range of color schemes. Moreover, because it is not complex, you can experiment with it on paper and try

The finished stencil after varnishing. The varnish emphasizes the off-white color of the paint. *Photo by David Arky.*

introducing additional elements. It is structured so you can use it as an overall pattern or simply as a border.

DEGREE OF DIFFICULTY Moderately easy

TIME REQUIRED 4–5 days: making stencils, ½ day; marking floor, ½ day; stencilling, 1½ days for two people or 3 days for one person; varnishing, 1 day plus drying time

MATERIALS
basic equipment, page 12
2 sheets .0075 acetate
1 sheet .010 acetate
compass
plumb line and chalk box
chalk pencil
metal measuring tape
2 stencil brushes (at least 1")
tissues
tack cloth
plastic drop cloth
white cotton socks and kneepads
turpentine or paint thinner
matte polyurethane varnish
paintbrush (2")

JAPAN COLORS
flake white
French yellow ochre
burnt umber

1. Making the Stencils

Set yourself up with a drawing board at least 24 inches by 24 inches and a glass cutting mat of the same size (the largest stencil will be this size). You will be making five stencils in all: the large cross, the smaller cross (assuming you have an area requiring the smaller design), the large circle for the corners, and two small circles for the center of each size of cross.

Enlarge the large cross motif as indicated, so that it measures 18 inches square, using plain or graph paper. The bars of the larger cross should be ⅜ inch wide.

Similarly, scale up the smaller cross on paper so that it measures 12 inches square. The bars for this cross should be ¼ inch wide.

To make the stencil circles, use a compass: the large corner circle should be 3⅞ inches in diameter, the larger central circle ⅝ inch in diameter, and the smallest circle ½ inch.

Using .0075 grade acetate, cut one piece 24 inches square for the larger design and one 16 inches square for the smaller design. Also cut 8-inch, 5-inch, and 4-inch square pieces for the circles.

Trace the enlarged designs with any registration lines onto the acetate with a technical drawing pen and permanent ink, using a metal ruler for the straight lines. Mark "Top" in the upper right-hand corner of each stencil on the side on which you have been tracing. Using your utility knife, cut all the stencils.

Using .010 acetate, cut two strips approximately 30 inches by 6 inches for the borders. Each strip should have a precut edge on one long side. You will paint against these edges to achieve a cleaner line for the border. Save leftover pieces of acetate to use for masking.

Apply liberal amounts of masking tape around the edges of the top side of each stencil and to one long edge and the two short ends of each border strip. (These pieces of masking tape lose their stickiness and must be frequently replaced.)

2. Marking Out the Floor

This design will fit easily into any shape of room. You can bend the border around corners, whatever their angle, and the procedure for marking out the floor is the same, whatever the shape.

Border First, measure 8 inches in from the baseboards all around the room and mark points on the floor with chalk. This will allow for a 2-inch space between the wall and the 6-inch width of border (two 1-inch stripes with a 4-inch space in between). Mark points on the floor 2 inches in from the baseboard at every corner. Then mark points 1 inch in from each of the previous points to indicate the outside stripe. Then mark points 4 inches in from the last points, and another set 1 inch in again for the inside stripe (see fig. 37). If you have a small alcove to include, as Cile did, continue marking the border around this area as well.

Using a plumb line and chalk box, start at the outsides and snap a chalk line between each of these points so that the entire border is mapped out and the ends of all the lines intersect (see fig. 37 again). Once you have put the chalk lines down, take care not to rub them out when walking over the floor as you continue marking.

Main floor When marking the main area of a floor into

Snapping the chalk line to mark out the grid on the floor. *Photo by David Arky.*

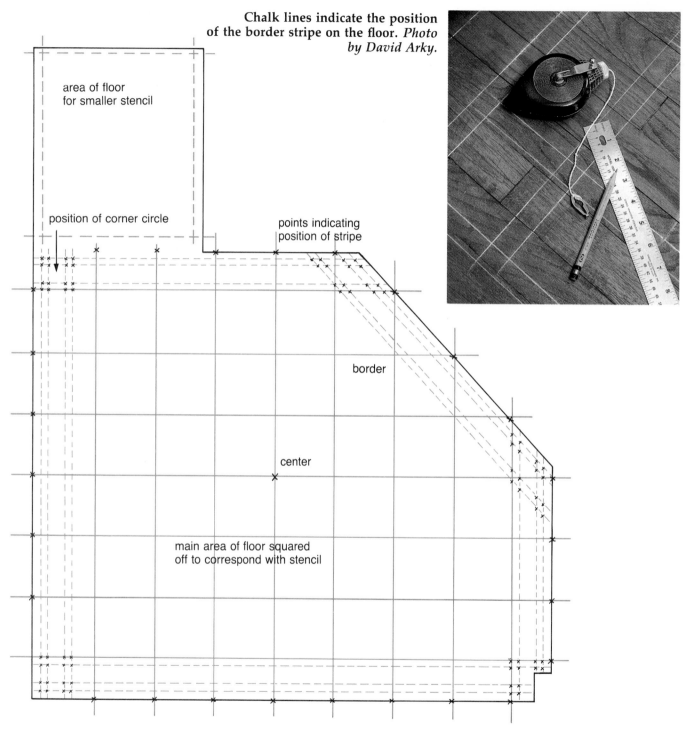

Chalk lines indicate the position of the border stripe on the floor. *Photo by David Arky.*

area of floor
for smaller stencil

position of corner circle

points indicating
position of stripe

border

center

main area of floor squared
off to correspond with stencil

*Figure 37 The marked-out
floor plan for Cile Lord's project*

squares, it is usual to start at the center and work out so that the pattern is evenly distributed. In this way, the pattern balances at each end of the floor—a fragment on one side is matched by a corresponding fragment on the opposite side. If you know that a pattern exactly fits the width of your room, you may choose to start at one side, but centering is still recommended because it will take care of any idiosyncrasies in the surrounding walls and fittings.

First find the center lengthwise and mark the floor into 18-inch sections to either side of this point. Mark the points at opposite ends of the floor and fill in with chalk lines. Then find the center widthwise and mark points 18 inches to each side of this point. Using the plumb line again, map out the floor in 18-inch squares (and partial squares at the edges). Check all measurements with a ruler as you go along, particularly the borders, which rely on the markings rather than a stencil. If you have an area of floor requiring the smaller design as well, mark this off in 12-inch squares in the same way (see fig. 37).

3. Applying the Stencils

Set up your work station away from the floor surface, in an area covered with a plastic drop cloth and newspapers. Mix the raw umber paint with a little thinner until it is the consistency of cream. Work the paint into the brush, removing the excess on a paper towel, and make a proof on paper if you like.

If you are stencilling single-handed, start with the borders. If two of you are working and the room is large enough, one can attack the borders while the other works on the main stencil. To stencil the borders, align the two long strips of acetate along either side of one marked-out stripe. Start in one corner and work out from there, blocking off the beginning of the border with a smaller piece of straight-edged acetate. Using a 1-inch stencil brush (or larger), apply the raw umber paint evenly between the strips. When you have covered this area, move the acetate strips and continue stencilling until you reach the end of one side, which also should be masked to ensure a clean edge. Turn the corner, masking off the stencilled end of the first stripe so that the paint is not applied twice in the corner. Continue stencilling in this way until the entire double border is complete.

Mix the paint for the stencil crosses, using about 15 parts flake white to 1 part French yellow ochre. Mix enough paint for the entire floor (about half a pint) and keep the mixed paint you are not using tightly sealed with cellophane wrap or foil. Make a paper proof or two to test the color and experiment until you get the strength of color you want.

Flake white is a lead-based pigment and therefore toxic. Its advantage is that it has the best covering power, which is important when stencilling light over dark. However, if you want to avoid using a toxic substance, you can substitute either zinc white or striping white.

For the stripe border, straight pieces of acetate mark out the area where the paint should be applied. *Photo by David Arky.*

Applying one of the crisscross stencils. *Photo by David Arky.*

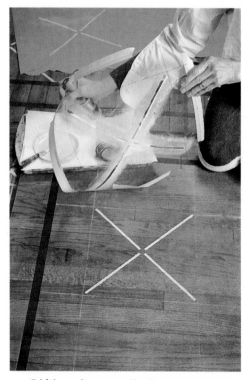

Lifting the stencil after it has been applied to reveal the clearly defined print. *Photo by David Arky.*

Work from the center outward when applying the cross stencils. When the floor is darker than the stencil color, as it is here, it is necessary to work the paint quite thoroughly when applying it through the stencil. After you have applied the first stencil, work to one side of it and then the other, alternating each time so that an edge of the stencil doesn't overlap a wet print. When you reach the border, mask it with acetate strips before you apply your stencil. Apply the smaller crosses in the same way if you are using them.

When the crosses are complete, continue with the cream paint and same brush and apply the large cream circles in each corner of the border, taking care to center them between the lines of the border pattern. Finally stencil in the small burnt umber dots in the center of each cream cross. *Note*: Allow two days for the stencilling to dry thoroughly.

4. Finishing Off

Carefully clean the floor surface with a vacuum cleaner and tack cloth. Test a tiny area of your stencilled floor with the varnish you intend to use to make sure that no bleeding occurs. With a 2-inch paintbrush, apply an even coat of varnish over the entire floor. The next day, apply a second coat. Allow two days' drying time for this second coat before walking on the floor.

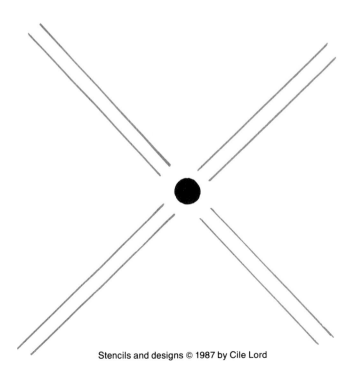

Stencils and designs © 1987 by Cile Lord

Enlarge 172%

Bibliography

ALBERS, JOSEF. *Interaction of Color*, rev. ed. New Haven, Conn., Yale University Press, 1975

BISHOP, ADELE, AND CILE LORD. *The Art of Decorative Stenciling*. New York, Viking Press, 1976. Rev. ed., Penguin Books, 1985.

EMMERLING, MARY ELLISOR. *Collecting American Country*. New York, Clarkson N. Potter, 1983.

FALES, DEAN A., JR. *American Painted Furniture 1660-1880*. Robert C. Bishop, ed. New York, E.P. Dutton, 1972.

FJELSTUL, ALICE BANCROFT, AND PATRICIA BROWN SCHAD, WITH BARBARA MARHOEFER. *Early American Wall Stencils in Color*. New York, E.P. Dutton, 1982. *More Early American Stencils in Color*. New York, E.P. Dutton, 1985.

FOBEL, JIM, AND JIM BOLEACH. *The Stencil Book*. New York, Holt, Rinehart and Winston, 1976.

GILLON, EDMUND V., JR. *Victorian Stencils for Design and Decoration*. New York, Dover Publications, 1968.

GLASS, FREDERICK JAMES. *Stencil Craft*. London, University of London Press, 1927.

INNES, JOCASTA. *Paint Magic*. New York, Van Nostrand Reinhold, 1981.

JEWETT, KENNETH, AND STEPHEN WHITNEY. *Early New England Wall Stencils*. New York, Harmony Books, 1968.

JENSEN, ROBERT, AND PATRICIA CONWAY. *Ornamentalism: The New Decorativeness in Architecture and Design*. New York, Clarkson N. Potter, 1982.

LE GRICE, LYN. *The Art of Stencilling*. New York, Clarkson N. Potter, 1987.

LIPMAN, JEAN, WITH EVE MEULENDYKE. *Techniques in American Folk Decoration*. New York, Dover Publications, 1972.

LIPMAN, JEAN, AND ALICE WINCHESTER. *The Flowering of American Folk Art: 1776-1876*. New York, Viking Press, 1974.

O'NEIL, ISABEL. *The Art of the Painted Finish*. New York, William Morrow, 1971.

STEPHENSEN, JESSIE. *From Old Stencils to Silk Screening*. New York, Charles Scribner's Sons, 1953.

WARING, JANET. *Early American Stencils on Walls and Furniture*. New York, Dover Publications, 1968. (Originally published as *Early American Wall Stencils, Their Origin, History, and Use*. New York, William R. Scott, 1942.)

Sources and Suppliers

Bentwood, Inc., P.O. Box 1676, Thomasville, GA 31792 (912) 226-1223. Shaker-style cheeseboxes, baskets, buckets, canisters, suitable for stencilling.

Adele Bishop Inc., P.O. Box 3349, Kinston, NC 28502-3349 (919) 527-4186. Precut stencils, japan paints, brushes, knives, stencil sheets and instruction books.

Arthur Brown & Brothers, 2 West 46th Street, New York, NY 10036 (212) 575-5555. All stencil supplies, including precut stencils, books, knives, paints, and acetate.

Classic Crafts, P.O. Box 267, Nazareth, PA 18064 (215) 759-3903. Theorem painting kits and patterns; bronzing powders and stencils for furniture.

Decorative Arts of Vermont, R.R. #1 Box 136, Dorset, VT 05251. All stencil supplies, including precut and ready-to-cut stencils, paints, brushes, and knives.

Dover Publications, 31 E. 2nd Street, Mineola, NY 11501. Publisher of a series of "cut & use" stencil books, printed on durable paper, including Pennsylvania Dutch, Art Nouveau, Victorian, Japanese, Art Deco, and border designs. Write for free catalog.

Illinois Bronze Paint Co., Lake Zurich, IL 60047 (312) 438-8201. Precut stencils, acrylic paints, fabric paints, brushes.

Janovic Plaza, 1292 First Avenue, New York, NY 10021. General paint supplies, as well as stencilling supplies.

Pavilion, 6a Howe Street, Edinburgh, Scotland; represented by Swift Morris Interiors, 1208 Washington Street, Hoboken, NJ 07030. Precut stencils.

Plaid Enterprises, 1649 International Boulevard, P.O. Drawer E, Norcross, GA 30091 (404) 923-8200. Precut stencils, paints, brushes, books, stencil supplies.

P.S. Creative Wood, 10931 Sallings Road, Knoxville, TN 37922 (615) 966-6137. Manufacturer of wooden accessories that work well with stencils.

Society for the Preservation of New England Antiquities, Harrison Gray Otis House, 141 Cambridge Street, Boston, MA 02114 (617) 227-3956. Moses Eaton stencil patterns, early American.

Stencil Designs Ltd., 1 Ellis Street, London SW1, England (01) 730-0728. Carolyn Warrender's shop, which carries precut stencils and stencilling supplies.

Stencil-Ease, P.O. Box 209, New Ipswich, NH 03071 (603) 878-3430. Large selection of precut stencils, paints, brushes, kits.

Stenciling Quarterly, The Magazine for Stenciling Enthusiasts, 6405 Atlantic Blvd., Norcross, GA 30071. Subscription rate $14 per year.

Stencil World, 8 West 19th Street, New York, NY 10011 (212) 675-8892. All stencil supplies, including precut stencils, stencil patterns, instruction books, paints, brushes. Send $2.50 for catalog.

Index